A MOTHER'S PLEASURE

A MOTHER'S PLEASURE

A Modern Guide to Redefining Motherhood

REGAN FIGG

the kind press

Copyright © 2022 Regan Figg
First published by the kind press, 2022

All rights reserved. No part of this book may be reproduced, stored in a retrieval system or transmitted in any form or by any means, electronic, mechanical photocopying, recording, or otherwise, without written permission from the author and publisher.

This publication contains the opinions and ideas of its author. It is intended to provide helpful, inspiration and informative material on the subjects addressed in the publication. While the publisher and author have used their best efforts in preparing this book, the material in this book is of the nature of general comment only. It is sold with the understanding that the author and publisher claim no responsibility to any person or entity for any liability, loss, or damage caused or alleged to be caused directly or indirectly as a result of the use, application, or interpretation of the material in this book. In the event that you use any of the information in this book for yourself, the author and the publisher assume no responsibility for your actions.

Cover design: Christa Moffitt, Christabella Designs
Editing: Georgia Jordan
Internal design: Nikki Matthews, Nikki Jane Design

Cataloguing-in-Publication entry is available from the National Library Australia.

ISBN: 978-0-6455237-0-6
ISBN: 978-0-6455237-1-3 ebook

For my children.

Inclusivity statement

In this book, I often speak in the language that is relevant to my experience of motherhood, sexuality and gender identity; I refer to myself as a woman and mother, mothering.

Should you identify differently to me, it is my hope that you can draw parallels with your own experience as I share my story. All forms of mother, and indeed all people, are welcome here.

Safety statement

Whilst I have studied human physiology, neuroscience, psychology, human biology and development (and other relevant subjects) through a Bachelor of Science (exercise science), neurolinguistic programming and yoga teaching, this book carries a collection of my personal experiences, ideas and embodied wisdom. It is not intended as a medical resource and shouldn't be treated as such.

A note on Mama Eros

In this book, you'll find reference to a figure I call Mama Eros. She is distinct from yet connected to the Greek god Eros, and is the personification of the goddess energy we all have within ourselves.

Contents

Dedication   *xiii*
Introduction   *xvii*
How to use this book   *xxiii*

Chapter One
Opening to pleasure 1

Chapter two
Full-spectrum Mother 11

Chapter three
From Maiden to Mother 21

Chapter four
Summoning your sensuality 29

Chapter five
The art of sensuality 43

Chapter six
Redefine desire 53

Chapter seven
Self-care and its insufficiencies 69

Chapter eight
Receive like a goddess 87

Chapter nine
Pleasure as a tool for
self-discovery and liberation 103

Chapter ten
Pleasure pathways 117

Chapter eleven
Through the body 131

Chapter twelve
Parenting with pleasure 151

Chapter thirteen
Anchoring pleasure 167

Chapter fourteen
Mama Eros 181

Resources	*189*
Acknowledgements	*193*
About the author	*197*

Dedication

As I sit here and type these words, I'm reminded of a time when I felt like I was drowning in motherhood. I felt like I wasn't good at doing any of the things, let alone *all* of the things. I was just doing the best I could being the wife, the housekeeper, the carrying-all-of-the-load-in-my-mind-and-on-my-heart kind of mama.

The person I was six years ago, as a new mother, wouldn't be able to recognise the person I am today. There's no way I ever thought I'd be able to cope with any more children after the first. I would never have thought I'd be able to have three in four and a half years, with the beautiful chaos of life around me, and feel settled—not that I have settled, but *feel* settled. Feel capable, and at peace, and mostly entertained by it all.

I am so proud of what I have done for myself, of who I have become. I am proud of myself for moving through those dark places six years ago and coming out the other side. I never thought any of them would lead to finding pleasure, dripping with children, a house that needs constant tidying (that I often ignore), a marriage that doesn't get a lot of airtime between all of the things but is deeply connected, and not a whole lot of time, energy or space for myself.

What I wish I could share with that woman five years ago!

I'd let her know that she would make it out alive, and learn to expand her capacity. Even when it feels like she's moving through the eye of the needle, it's part of the process that enables her to be stretched further than she ever has before, and find peace, pleasure and space on the other side.

I'd tell her that she makes her life better than it's ever been, that she discovers so many ways to find presence, to feel connected to life in the most sensual of ways.

I'd tell her that she redefines her desires, discovers how to truly receive and resource herself, and finds a pleasure-filled path back home to herself—not because she was ever 'lost', but simply because she wants to be with the woman who lives there.

So this book is for her, the woman I was five years ago in the depths of depletion. For the woman who, if only she had been gifted some of the wisdom in this book to soak into her system say, over a weekend in a hot tub with a candle and some stillness, wouldn't have needed to suffer as much as she did.

But having suffered, she now has a gift to give to the world, and to you, dear reader. And for that I will be forever thankful.

Whether or not you are in dark and challenging places in your motherhood journey, may you be able to take what

A MOTHER'S PLEASURE

I've learned, weave it through your life like a golden thread, and bring more light into your journey, more pleasure into your parenting, and more enjoyment into the everyday. For life is to be lived with pleasure, and I hope that by the end of this book you can feel that in your bones, and know it to be true beyond a shadow of a doubt.

Introduction

My pursuit of pleasure was born from a place of darkness and struggle.

Before becoming a mother I was an exercise physiologist, a professional dancer, a health and wellness coach, and a yoga and meditation teacher. I was the eternal optimist—with no history of mental health struggles—known for my upbeat, energetic personality.

Four months into motherhood, my son was waking around ten times a night, and this went on for weeks. He started to sleep again, but my body had forgotten how. Three months later I was diagnosed with postnatal depression and anxiety. I had insomnia and suicidal ideation.

Pleasure was not the access point I had envisioned for my recovery, but it's where I began the journey back home to myself.

I began to foster a deeper relationship with my body and develop my understanding of my mind. I began to redefine what felt good for me depending on the available time and energy I had, and let go of a lot of my preconceived ideas about motherhood and what it looked like to enjoy motherhood.

Within ten months we had moved interstate. We had very minimal family around and no friends, and I discovered I was pregnant again. This time I devoted my resources to not just making sure that I was ok; I went on an exploration to discover what I could do to ensure that I was *good*.

I began to realise that if I could follow my compass of pleasure, I could feel good. I devoted myself to seeking, finding and receiving all the pleasures that life had to offer me. A coffee in the sunshine, a massage with a napping baby in a pram, a yoga class, lunch out with newfound friends, intimacy with my husband—from spooning on the lounge to erotic pleasure when I was ready.

I managed to prevent any perinatal mood disorders from arising again after my second child was born. I also realised that this devotion to pleasure was not only helping me to feel good; it was actually a tool for personal growth, and a whole range of things you'll explore in this book.

Fast forward two years and I birthed our third baby. This time a girl, birthed in the most ecstatic birth that I attributed to my new pleasure-centred, self-focussed way of existence. This time it was less about being ok, or even feeling good. This time I decided to explore the question, *Could I feel more than good? Could I feel fucking amazing? Could I make every moment of every day ecstatic? Could I squeeze all the juice there is out of life, with three children (under five)?*

It was another peeling back of a layer within. Where society said that each child I birthed meant less time, less space, less money, less connection, less enjoyment, less intimacy, I decided to respectfully disagree. I decided that 'babies bring abundance' (thank you Denise Duffield-Thomas for that quote) and it's been nothing short of it.

What I hadn't realised was that there would be many barriers to break through, many layers to be shed, to receive the pleasure I was prioritising.

I soon discovered that it wasn't just me who had barriers to pleasure. I discovered how deeply we, as women and mothers, are conditioned and socialised (amongst other things) to be driven from our desires and pushed from our pleasure. I discovered that there is a lot of work to be done in this area of motherhood—important work—and this book is part of my contribution to the conversation.

I no longer see motherhood as a place where you lose yourself. I see it as a place of opportunity. A field of gold where we get to redefine what actually feels good for us, realise what is most important to us. We get to decide how we want to feel in connection with ourselves and others, and have the opportunity to become deeply intimate in these connections.

It is a time where naturally, a Pandora's box of unconscious beliefs is opened for us to keep, or rewrite if the stories don't serve us. We get to craft a life that is more heaven-on-earth than we had ever even intended. We get to redefine our desires and let them find us, but first, just like Pandora's box, we must open.

You'll discover that having a life full of pleasure does not mean sacrificing what matters to you most—whether that be time with your children, your career, your business, or your health. This is a concern created from our conditioning; I invite you to stay with me. Stay connected to your pleasure. Stay devoted to your desires. Stay with this book through each chapter as we go deep into deprogramming and unveiling.

You'll discover that pleasure is both the tool and the by-product of self-discovery, personal growth and being devoted to your desires, and often, we must pass through the shadow to get there. At times it may feel really confronting and uncomfortable, so this is your advance reminder that you're not broken, doing it wrong or not trying hard enough. It means you are on the way. And to begin, just as you have opened this book not knowing what you'd find inside, we must open to pleasure and trust that what we find along the journey is exactly what we need.

Whether you want to be part of the pleasure revolution that's on its way, or simply experience a more pleasurable version of motherhood, the choice is yours. Either way, by the time you reach the end of this book, your life will have changed for the better.

You will have found pockets of pleasure you never knew existed, you will love more about yourself and your body than perhaps you have your entire life. You will have remembered your birthright to ecstasy, sensuality, pleasure, enjoyment, satisfaction and fulfilment. Most importantly, you will have begun to reclaim parts of yourself that you might not have ever realised existed.

The threads of gold within this book are likely to lift you out of depletion, unfulfilment and dissatisfaction, and support you to seek, find, explore, create, and maybe even

A MOTHER'S PLEASURE

construct a new way of being in motherhood. Perhaps you will help develop a new paradigm for our future mothers—should you choose to.

How to use this book

This book combines memoir, cultural commentary and self-help. It includes stories from myself and from other women (with their permission) exploring the pursuit of pleasure in motherhood. Practices, prompts, invitations to enquiry, and rituals are incorporated—typically at the end of each chapter—to help you integrate the learnings into your body and your life.

My suggestion is that you complete the practical components while the relevant chapter is still fresh in your mind before moving on to the next chapter, but if you find that you have the opportunity to devour more than one chapter in one sitting and don't want to stop the flow of reading, you can always come back to the practical components and they will still serve their purpose.

I have intentionally not created space for you to complete work in the book, in case you would like to pass it on to a friend who could use more pleasure in their life. I suggest you select a journal to use alongside this book (but don't let not having one be the reason you don't start).

This book is ideally consumed from start to finish.

However, if you feel called to open to a particular chapter, this will serve you as well.

Move through this book in the way that I am now inviting you to move through life: as you please, driven by desire, prioritising pleasure. This is part of your pleasure practice now.

Each time you prepare to open to this book, ask, *How can I make this more pleasurable?* This may mean wrapping yourself in a blanket, sliding on some slippers, running a bath or moving outside into the sun—solo or with your littlies alongside you. Partner this book with a creamy coffee or refreshing juice, a slice of cake or a nourishing meal, with incense or essential oils. Pleasure is a practice, a learned skill you craft.

On your pathway to pleasure you may be confronted with moments of discomfort or unpleasant realisations. Go gently; be open to what comes up without judgement.

And before we dive in, ask yourself, *What's my intention for this journey?* And can you decide right this moment that your intention will manifest, and be anchored in more powerfully, with the turning of each page?

We begin here, with the turn of this page, the start of your new life, centred in pleasure.

Let's normalise a mother prioritising her pleasure. Share the activities you're loving from *A Mother's Pleasure* on your socials for others to discover and tag @Regan_Figg

Chapter One
OPENING TO PLEASURE

Pleasure is not reserved for the privileged—for the ones who have spare time, spare money, spare energy. You get to experience pleasure because you are YOU. You are here. You are human. You are alive, and that is all that is required. If you have a body and this book, be prepared for more pleasure.

I wrote this book in the hopes that I can help you open more fully to yourself through the portal of pleasure. You might have picked up this book because you are on the cusp of your own pleasure revolution. You're ready to reclaim that part of you that has been shamed, abandoned and admonished. That part of you that has been ignored, condemned and suppressed—perhaps at the hands of yourself.

Perhaps you're no longer willing to accept that a woman

connecting to her body, experiencing pleasure, is wrong. You no longer want to be part of a world where this conditioning is handed down. You are feeling a simmering inner-wisdom whisper that says, *I don't want this for me, or for those who come after. I am done. It stops here. I am choosing me, and in choosing me, I am choosing a new world. And I am choosing to do it with pleasure.*

The kind of woman drawn to this book, and drawn to my work, might not be the kind you or our society expects. She is not a woman with extra time on her hands who's just after some kind of passing superficial sensation. She is not a woman who is disconnected from her children, or looking only to serve herself. She is not some kind of sacrifice-all-for-my-pleasure-or-else person—not that any of these constitutions are right or wrong. This is simply an observation.

The type of woman drawn to this book, drawn to the way of pleasure, is this: a mindful mama who wants to create deeply connected relationships with those she loves; a nurturing home life; and a better, loving world not just for herself, but for her children to grow up in. She wants to be the best mother and woman she can be, and she's been dutifully following the rules. But now she's realising the rules have her feeling a little (or a lot) sad or exhausted, and getting a little (or a lot) shouty with her children and loved ones.

She is awakening to the bullshit patriarchal narrative and societal beliefs that a mother's pleasure is shameful; that it's frivolous, irresponsible, selfish, disgraceful. That it is to be delayed until she's been productive, her desires denied until everyone else's are met. That if she is a good mother, she should already be satiated.

There's a part of her that knows her pleasure is sacred. That experiencing pleasure and enjoying herself is her birthright. It's her power. It is *full* of grace.

This is your invitation to discover more of YOU through the portal of pleasure. This book invites you to explore your relationship with desire and pleasure (often unconsciously crafted by outside influences), and how we can foster a relationship with desire, pleasure and receiving that allows us to feel unapologetically *alive*, and nourish every aspect of our life.

It's discovering what's stopping us from walking a pleasure-filled path now, and learning the art of experiencing life through a lens of ecstasy.

It's summoning sensuality and receiving like a goddess.

It's parenting with and anchoring in pleasure, not in spite of being a mother, but because of it.

It's everything I've explored, discovered, integrated and embodied with three little babes, often during times of limited support.

It's from my pleasure journey to your pleasure awakening.

It's layered but it's not laborious.

The practices are timeless, not time consuming.

It gets to be the way for you.

The portal of pleasure

There are some things that I want you to know about this journey of pleasure that you're stepping into—either trepidatiously or with full force, or somewhere in between. The first is that pleasure will begin to subtly loosen the binds that may have constricted much of your life and let ease and joy stream in.

It's like when you have a tangled necklace—pleasure is the thing that does the loosening of the knots first so you can get a better perspective of which threads are really tightly knotted and which threads you need to pull to untangle it all. There might be some difficult moments in the untangling, but you will get to adorn yourself with gold again, and the loosening that you do throughout makes the process so much easier and enjoyable.

What I want you to know is that a mother's pleasure is an act of revolt against the grain of patriarchal culture. You're not crazy for feeling like you're overwhelmed doing everything that you're 'supposed' to, and then left wondering, *What else is there?* Feeling like there's something missing.

As Glennon Doyle perfectly said on her podcast We Can Do Hard Things:

> Those days of three little ones at home were the most holy and hardest ... Every day was far too much and not even close to enough. I was somehow constantly both completely overwhelmed and thoroughly underwhelmed at the same time.

Flowing within us and our society is an unconscious undercurrent of societal, historical and cultural narratives that discourages a mother from her pleasure, makes it difficult for her to access it, and causes discomfort when she does.

What I really want you to know is that pleasure is an invitation home to yourself.

When we deny our desires, when we suppress our pleasures, when we try to fit the perfect-mother mould, we abandon our full selves. The way home is through the portal of pleasure—but sometimes, before we get there, we meet stories of not being deserving enough, of not having achieved enough, or not being 'allowed'.

Sometimes we yield to the stories because it just all feels too uncomfortable when we attempt to 'indulge' ourselves in what is our birthright. And so we move further and further from knowing, loving and honouring our true selves, which moves us further from our joy, happiness and fulfilment—further from experiencing deeper intimacy in relationship with others and with life itself.

Where power lies

If you feel like you are part of the change that motherhood needs, I am SO pleased that you're here. I see this book as the bridge between the old paradigm of martyred motherhood and the new paradigm of motherhood that is self-focussed.

I see this book less as an act of revolt against the patriarchal version of motherhood, and more a divine devotion to pleasuring our way out of a tightly restrained system, into an open field of golden light.

After all, we reclaim our power not by our 'Fuck you' to the patriarchy; we reclaim our power by our 'Fuck YES' to pleasure.

Whilst I've had my times of flippin' the bird to patriarchy, this becomes more about 'Fuck(ing) you' and less about pleasing me.

And pleasing me, and my pleasure? A mother's pleasure? That is where the power lies. You just wait and see.

Activity
Defining your pleasure

When I talk about pleasure, I am talking about the feel-good state we experience in our body—whether that be through laughing, sensual pathways, sexual experiences or other means.

I invite you to consider what pleasure means to you. What's your definition of pleasure? What does it look like? What does it feel like? What does it taste, smell and sound like?

In your journal, jot down everything you

can think of that aligns with that definition in your life. In other words, what brings you pleasure?

Here we begin your pleasure prescription, your Feel-Good Guide: a list of everything you can think of that brings you pleasure. Keep it with you, or on the fridge/mirror/wherever, and continue to add to it as you journey through this book.

We will dive deeper into exploring your relationship to pleasure in an upcoming chapter. But for now, I invite you to consider what pleasure means for you.

Perhaps the first thing that comes to mind is sexual pleasure, but when you go deeper, you realise you relate pleasure to peace, fun, enjoyment, or sensations outside of the sexual realm.

If you're not sure, or feel disconnected from pleasure and can't come up with anything, don't worry. There's nothing wrong with you and you certainly are not alone. See this as your starting point with a big potential for pleasure.

Give yourself at least ten minutes to journal from that woman deep within who craves a more tactile, pleasure-filled life.

Here are some prompts you might like to use; see what streams out:

- Where are you at now on your pleasure journey and where do you see yourself going?
- Where do you want to be with pleasure?
- What's it like there? And what's the difference from where you are now?

Lastly, I invite you to declare that you are intentionally open to pleasure. That you are open to your desires. That you are open to any of the binds that tightly hold your life loosening up and falling down, and letting pleasure stream in from everywhere.

Offer yourself a mantra as your move through your days:

> Open. Open. Open. I am open to pleasure.
> I am open and willing to experience more pleasure.
> I am open to welcoming the pleasured version of myself into life.

Choose or create whatever version feels good for you.

Let's open.

This is your invitation
to discover more
of YOU through
the portal of pleasure.

Chapter Two

FULL-SPECTRUM MOTHER

When my first son was two, he called me by name. He even had his preschool carer write it on the back of a little finger-painted turtle.

I relished him calling me by my name. And imagining the conversation he had with his carer, directing her to write *Regan* on his all-purple turtle. For me, it felt like such a compliment.

It meant he saw me.

He saw a person. Not a role. Not a socialised figure. Not 'just' a mother.

Me!

All of me. All wrapped up in my name.

For I am Regan, not "just" his mum.

Being seen as Regan by my son meant being seen as the full-spectrum woman that I am, over the singular role of mother that our society perpetuates—where a woman feels required to abandon, reject, suppress and conceal parts of herself to fit the socially acceptable mould of 'Mother'.

To me, it was evidence that the fully-expressed, whole person that I am had been witnessed and honoured. And as women, isn't that all we ever truly desire? To be witnessed and seen as our whole selves, without all the masks, and be loved as we are? Perhaps something we perpetuate as mothers—wearing masks and concealing parts of ourselves only to be deemed 'just a mum' by society?

Becoming Mother

By taking on the name Mum, by becoming Mother, it is like we unknowingly commit to abiding by the societal 'rules' that come with that.

We conceal the parts that are wild, angry, playful, self-focussed, sexual, rageful, emotional, regretful, sad, ambitious and more.

We step ourselves into that box titled *Mother*, leaving parts of the woman that we are outside that box. And we only reunite with those other parts of ourselves in 'me time'—behind closed doors; when the kids are in bed; when the kids are older; in the moments we aren't with our children, caregiving, nurturing and selflessly sacrificing ourselves for them.

For we know the person we 'should' be as a mother, and it certainly isn't our full-spectrum selves.

This is something that we have been groomed for since

we were small children. It is something that has been socialised into us from a very early age and ramps up as we near the years of potentially becoming a mother, then emerges again as we move through the rite of passage from maiden to mother.

When we acknowledge ourselves as Mother we are also aware, on some level, that we are assigning ourselves many other characteristics—such as gentle, nurturing, selfless, devoted, housekeeper, ever-present, self-sacrificing, balanced and caring (whilst concealing others less welcomed by society). And we are all those things ... until we're not. Until the very society that created this identity for us fails to provide the support, connection and resources required to be only those things, no matter how much we want to embody them, no matter how much we try to fit.

For in the end, we are human. We are full-spectrum women, mothering.

The tide is turning

When we try to resist the universal law of polarity—where there are always equal and opposite parts within ourselves and our world—when we abandon parts of ourselves to try and fit the mould, we inevitably 'slip up' and parts of our whole self shine through. We can find ourselves comparing ourselves to other mothers and the image of the perfect mother. We are left unfulfilled, unsatisfied and disappointed, carrying a sense of shame and disillusion, wondering why we can't just get our act together like other 'normal mums'.

Logically we know that we are not 'just a mum' and might even detest the phrase—but still, it can slip into our minds, slip out from our mouths like some default setting that we keep meaning to fix but don't quite know how. I suspect that when we use the phrase, we feel (unconsciously or otherwise) that we are required to leave parts of ourselves behind in order to fit into the impossible mould that our society has glorified and pushed onto us. And we are shamed if we do not stick to our 'role', like it's some kind of performance.

Looking back through my own lineage of mothers, I suspect they didn't feel safe to be their full-spectrum selves either, with women in the fifties being advised to pray their way out of frustration and anger. Thankfully for us, the tide is turning; the feminine is rising and so too is our conscious awareness of what we bring to the world's table. For we have great influence on the way our world evolves—through our children.

I believe we are one generation away from heaven on earth, and part of that is a cultural shift where all people, especially mothers, are resourced, capable and encouraged to access, receive, experience and respond to life in a way that is pleasurable for them, whatever that looks like.

The impossible identity

We have been socialised into this role and these expectations whether we're aware of it or not. Whether we believe in the rules and expectations or not, whether we are 'doing a good job' or not. No one is immune to it.

This is why mothers can find judgement within mothers groups and open society: there is a societal expectation of who a mother is and how she behaves and how she should spend her time. There is policing of the culturally crafted identity of the mother and no one is more judgemental of a mother than herself, for she has been in training for this her whole life.

So I started to question what the title 'Mother' represents, and began to construct my own version of what it means to be a mother, outside of what has already been insufficiently crafted by our culture.

I think the reason that I like it when my child calls me by my name is because it feels like a rejection of the impossible identity that society has pushed upon me. It feels like a nod to my full-spectrum self. The woman from which the mother is born, not the woman hidden somewhere in the depths of the mother, as our culture would prefer.

Your full-spectrum self

With this chapter I hope to offer you an opportunity to consider what parts of yourself you've shut down, repressed, abandoned, ignored or dismissed. To consider who you would be if you were free from society's expectations and conditioning, and were your full-spectrum self. To fuel yourself by being self-focussed, self-aware and desire-driven, because if you've not already put your finger on it, trying to be someone you're not is fucking exhausting. No mother's got time for that!

It is my experience, and that of the mothers I work with, that when we stop rejecting parts of ourselves, energy ignites itself from within, fulfilment flows back to us, satisfaction starts to be uncovered, compassion and kindness arise, intimacy blossoms, and pleasure starts to drip into our experience of motherhood, and all facets of our lives.

When we strive to be the selfless, self-sacrificing mother, we reject the parts of ourselves that seek and receive pleasure. We abandon the parts of ourselves that often began our motherhood journey in the first place. We nurture ourselves last, if at all. We shut down our sexuality, our desires and our drive for pleasure, consciously or unconsciously. We police ourselves, or experience policing of the perfect-mother myth by others, through one very effective way of keeping us 'in line' with society's expectations. Any guesses how?

We'll dive in there next.

Activity
Rediscovering you

Take some time to reflect on the following questions and jot down some answers in your journal.

A MOTHER'S PLEASURE

- Are there parts of you that you suspect or know you keep to yourself for fear of straying from societal norms?

- Are there parts of your life that ignite a burning rage? Or perhaps a smouldering, low-level 'no fucks left' energy? When you reach those points where you're in a state of rage, or have 'no fucks left to give', I invite you to list all of the things that are igniting these feelings.

  > This is your body showing you what is in opposition to your full-spectrum self and your truth. What changes can you make to navigate back toward your truth?

- Who would you be if you embraced your full-spectrum self? What would your life be like? What's different between where you're at now and your full-spectrum self? What are some things available to you now that you could weave into your world to begin bridging this gap? Is it being more silly, having more fun, saying no to what feels like obligation, saying yes to what feels like YOU, letting your rage out in a healthy way, leaning into pleasure?

We are human.
We are full-spectrum
women, mothering.

Chapter three

FROM MAIDEN TO MOTHER

The one very effective way of keeping us in line with society's expectations of the perfect mother, that has us policing ourselves and each other (even if unconsciously), is through shame.

Even if we feel like shame and socialisation have only had a slight imprint on us, it can be hard to advocate for ourselves and our pleasure in a culture where a woman becomes increasingly invisible the further she moves from maiden to mother. The deeper a woman descends into the realms of being seen by society as unsexy, unattractive and unglamorous, the more she experiences an internal sense of self-disgust and distrust.

Recently, a friend of mine declared on her Insta stories how grateful she was that she didn't have children. She'd had such a productive day in her business, felt so alive from the time she had for creative expression, was relishing in the freedom of moving through her day as she pleased, and was appreciating how—after having a rose-petal bubble bath—she could laze around on the couch in a towel for as long as she liked, until she went to her exercise session that night, followed by dinner out with friends.

I loved that she was relishing her life, even if it was hard to not feel jealous, as I was dripping with three small children in a pandemic lockdown. But mostly it made me realise that she was aware of what we're speaking of in this chapter.

My friend is aware of what her life is supposed to look like if she becomes a mother, because 'obviously' she wouldn't be able to do all of those things. Perhaps she assumed she'd be a slave to her children and her home all day long, as our society continues to reinforce and remind us. She knows that as a mother she couldn't be self-focussed. Mothers aren't supposed to have time for creative expression, exercise, and lazing around in a towel as long as they like.

But what if it didn't have to be that way? What if we had the tools, resources and support required to have all of those things in our life, if that's what we desired? What if our children were watching us and learning a new idea of what it is to be a mother?

Increasing your capacity

Another thing came to mind when my child-free friend was speaking on her Insta stories: she hadn't realised the ability we have to increase our capacity as mothers (something I hadn't realised before becoming Mother, either).

Before I became a mother, I just assumed that whatever energetic, emotional, physical and intellectual skills and bandwidth I started out with, I was stuck with. I hadn't realised that it was possible to increase your capacity to hold emotion, to collapse time, to be more receptive, to feel more.

For example, no longer do I require a ninety-minute yoga session to feel a sense of peace, spaciousness, and connection to self. Don't get me wrong, I wouldn't turn it down, but I can now find those things in two minutes of silence in the sunshine with a coffee. I can find those things in little moments—little pockets that I never even knew existed before I had children.

I'm not just talking about being more efficient, although that's possible. I'm talking about increasing your capacity for awareness and receptivity. This goes for enjoyment and pleasure too.

Rewriting the narrative

When our second son was almost two, Jake (my husband) and I were sitting around the fire on a Friday evening at the start of autumn. We'd just finished up a backyard barbecue, the boys were exploring the garden with a torch, and the two of us were able to have a conversation without being interrupted for a good three to five minutes.

(Now we are able to achieve intimacy and connection

in just a few minutes, instead of believing we require romantic weekends away or full evenings out. Again, I certainly wouldn't turn these down, but it's gratifying to know that we've been able to increase our capacity to be piercingly present and deeply connected when we have a few minutes to ourselves.)

We were considering not having any more children. Life was pretty good and we were grateful to have two happy, healthy, ever-wild boys.

Well, we conceived our third child that week. When I discovered we were pregnant, I spent the first twenty-four hours crying. Grieving for the perceived time, money, attention and energy that we were about to lose to another season of newborn-baby life. It started to feel hopeless, until I realised that I was subscribing to society's narratives and not my own, and reminded myself that I could choose my experience. That I could create a new narrative different from the one I had thought was the truth, like I'd done so many times before.

So I began to find evidence for the reality I wanted to experience in my life. Surely there were other families with three children who were living in a way that I wanted to. And if it was possible for them, it was possible for us.

Babies bring abundance

Before having children, did you feel like you were tired and didn't have any time? Were you conscious of your finances? Then after having a child, did you still manage to find time, space, energy and finances?

Things shift, and transform, and rearrange.

I realised that I'd thought I had limited time, energy, money when we just had the one baby, and after we had our second, I was able to find pockets of time, space and energy that I didn't know existed. I realised that it was possible to find or create more time, more energy, more money, more abundance, more connection, more of whatever I wanted.

So whilst I was pregnant for the third time in four years, I decided that this baby would bring abundance, and I would live in a state of overflow. Abundance of time, energy, space, money, support … whatever I wanted. And what's so crazy is that it *has* been our reality, to the extent that—in the middle of a pandemic—my husband got a new job the week our daughter was born, and ended up doing that job from home for seven months, paid, until his organisation deemed it safe for their workers to return to site.

Activity
Your desired reality

The point of this chapter is: you don't have to subscribe to a certain kind of motherhood, or a certain kind of reality, simply because of societal norms. You don't have to switch to a state of scarcity because the cultural narrative is that the more children you have, the more you lose (time, money, space, energy, freedom).

When you know about how we've been conditioned to live, and what we've internalised as truth, and how we've been socialised to fit into one particular narrative, you begin to realise that the prescribed reality is just one option, one possibility, out of an endless number of possibilities that can be true for you.

I invite you to pull out your journal and consider the following prompts.

- Think back to my maiden friend earlier in the chapter. When you reflect on your maiden life compared with your mother life, what comes up for you? Remembrance, appreciation, resentment, annoyance, jealousy, desire, humility?

- Visualise yourself living life like my maiden friend—following your desires and focussing on yourself—but also being a mother to children. Does it feel deplorable? Unrealistic? Not allowed? Selfish? Exciting? Free? I invite you to write it all down without judgement. Here you'll begin to see the tip of the iceberg of your socialisation. (Later in the book we'll discover the depths of that iceberg, and explore how to melt away what isn't helpful in the chapter 'Pleasure as a tool for self-discovery and liberation'.)

You don't have to subscribe to a certain kind of motherhood, or a certain kind of reality, simply because of societal norms.

Chapter four
SUMMONING YOUR SENSUALITY

One sunny, toddler-free autumn morning in Melbourne, I was relishing a beautiful coffee date with a good friend in a big open park in Cheltenham. In a moment of appreciating our conversation and friendship, the warmth on my back and the greenery of the park swallowing us up, I also noticed the smell of laundry detergent coming from a woman passing us a few meters away.

'Oh god,' I said, 'I love the smell of whatever washing detergent she's using!'

Having been pregnant before, my girlfriend (knowing we weren't planning on having any more children) laughed and said, 'OMG, you're totally pregnant again!'

I went to the chemist on the way home that day, and it turns out I was.

Feminine and masculine energies

If you've experienced pregnancy before, chances are you will be acutely aware of how heightened your body's senses can be, and therefore how connected you can be to your body.

Smell is sharpened. Taste is intensified. We are more sensitive to touch.

We see and experience the world through a heightened sensory and somatic lens.

By the time you've fallen pregnant, you've probably spent most of your adult life, if not your entire life, operating predominantly from your masculine energy instead of your feminine energy.

In our society, we are encouraged to live life in a masculine way—to 'maintain momentum'; achieve; be competitive and goal oriented; operate from the mind; move fast; be direct, linear, angular, hard; have order, focus and control; be rational and logical. By contrast, the feminine is cyclical; process and collaboration oriented; body focussed; slow, soft, round, expressive and emotional; akin to chaos, spontaneity and surrender.

As feminine beings (if that's what you resonate with), we have finite amounts of masculine energy; this is why when we operate predominantly from our masculine, especially over long periods of time, we can end up burnt out, overwhelmed, 'up in our heads', numb and disconnected from our body, with limited access to our intuition.

Being naturally 'forced' into our feminine throughout pregnancy and the rite of passage into motherhood is such divine design. It helps a woman reconnect to her body, her feminine energy, her emotions and her intuition more deeply. This gives her the ability to surrender, trust herself, focus on nurturance, express herself and be with emotion and more, which are all such important abilities for birth and in the early postpartum period.

It can feel really uncomfortable to tap back into your feminine essence if you haven't been there in a while. Beginning to feel again, when perhaps you haven't felt in a very long time, can be unsettling and create resistance.

It can also feel like you're failing, not 'keeping up', being lazy and unproductive because the feminine is more about *being* and the masculine (and what you're likely most accustomed to) is more about *doing*. In this masculine-obsessed culture, when we're not seen as productive, we can feel unworthy, incompetent, less valuable. This is one of the reasons our culture does not value mothers and the role they play in raising the next generation.

Introducing sensuality

Society only values us when we are being productive, achieving goals and moving fast towards something. These are all traits of the masculine. We have a masculine-obsessed culture—makes sense when we're living in a patriarchal society. There is little to no reverence for the feminine—for the slow, the cyclical, the surrender. The masculine is celebrated for its ability to be rational and logical, to control and be mind-centric, while being emotional, expressive and creative (all attributes of the feminine) is not as celebrated.

Think of all the times you were put down for being 'too sensitive', 'a drama queen' or 'crazy' for following illogical intuition. We can look to what's taught in schools and at standard salaries to see what is valued in our society.

But the feminine deserves reverence and celebration. The feminine is the energy that brings life to the earth. The feminine is the high-level creative frequency that transforms numbness into desire and inspiration. It is life-force energy—tenderly fierce, capable of moving mountains. And yet it is squashed and shushed in our patriarchal society; shamed and repressed.

What does this have to do with sensuality, I hear you ask? I bet you came to this chapter with a bit of excitement, thinking you might be able to feel more, be more sensual, or ignite your libido, and here I am reminding you of the ever-oppressing patriarchy—not exactly foreplay.

One thing to remember is that sensuality is not sexuality. It can be a pathway to sexuality, but ultimately the two are separate. You can have a sensual experience with your morning coffee—chances are if you're in the trenches of sleep deprivation, it might look pretty darn sexy to you, but ultimately it's not a sexual experience.

Sensuality can be brought about, and found, in every moment of every day. It requires little to no investment of time, money or energy, but it does require your investment in attention. Attention to what is in the here and now, the present moment, has the greatest potential for connecting us with the tactile ecstasy of life itself.

Experiencing life through a lens of ecstasy

So what does sensuality have to do with the enthusiasm our society has for a masculine way of living?

When we are operating from the masculine, we are operating from the mind. If we are operating from the mind, we are not operating from the body, or 'in our bodies'. If we are not operating from the body, we cannot summon sensuality.

According to the Macquarie Dictionary, to be sensual is to be 'inclined to the gratification of the senses', and we cannot access our senses if we cannot land into and connect with our body.

In this chapter, you will be offered some practices to deepen your connection with your body, including one simple and effective sensuality practice that requires minimal time and energy but elicits great benefit and impact.

The more connected you are to your body:

- the easier it is to channel your intuition (a mother's superpower)
- the more you trust your body and its innate wisdom (perfect for birthing and the early days as a mother)
- the easier it is to navigate the emotions of pregnancy and the postpartum period
- the easier it is to regulate your nervous system, and therefore regulate your children's nervous systems

- the greater capacity you have for holding your emotions and those of your children
- the better you are at making decisions
- the better you can sense where your boundaries lie
- the better you're able to notice when you're going into a stress response

All of these capabilities are fundamental to experiencing life through a lens of ecstasy, where pleasure is woven into the fabric of your being, and the way you move through motherhood.

And just in case you're not sold on moving out of your head and into your body, let me be very clear: your body is the portal to pleasure. Pleasure is experienced through the body. If you're reading this book, and you want more pleasure in your life, it's time to descend below the neck.

Reconnect with your body

So let's go there. Let's make friends with our body and honour her for all that she has done and will do for us. Let's honour her for everything she has been through and gotten us through, what she's experienced in getting our children to us. What miracles have been created in us or through us.

Also take a moment for any of the ways you may have betrayed your body in the past. Perhaps you ignored her, abused her in some way or another. And now realise that she is still there, waiting for you to be present with her, to experience everything the world has to offer, through her. To see, to feel, hear, taste and smell each moment with.

(In the next chapter we will learn how to soften into our feminine even more, and open our pathways to pleasure even further.)

So, place one hand where your womb space is and one hand on your heart. Close your eyes and take a deep breath in and out, and then ask her, your body—*Are you ready to reconnect? Are you ready to deepen our connection? To move through our next chapter of this journey of motherhood together?*

It's ok to feel unsure, or uncomfortable, or even grief or sadness now. It is all welcome here. You are safe. You are held. You are loved.

Once you hear your *Yes,* know that that voice, the voice of your body, is always there for you. I cannot wait for you to experience what is to come of this deepening of intimacy between you and her.

Waking up to your senses

When I started playing around with this sensuality practice, there was a time I was getting our boys in the car on a freezing Melbourne morning. It had already been an intense morning; we had dashed out of the house, leaving behind the breakfast mess, sure the Weet-Bix would be concrete in the bowls by the time we got back.

The boys were only young, not quite four and two yet,

and they were going through quite a testing 'getting in the car' stage. By the time I got them both in their seats, and me in mine, and saw that we were going to be late to where we were going, I stopped to remind myself to sensualise …

There are two scenarios that could have happened here:

Scenario one

I put on my seatbelt and gripped the steering wheel, shoulders tense. Focussed on the end goal of our destination, I felt stressed and rushed. I took short breaths, probably getting annoyed by the noise in the back and the red lights. I probably drove too fast and reached our destination flustered and bothered.

Scenario two

I got into my seat and took a deep breath, feeling the support of the seat holding me. I put on some music I love, and pulled out as my shoulders relaxed.

As we drove, I looked around to see that the beautiful cherry blossoms were out. I could smell my coffee in the cup holder next to me, savouring the taste of it at the next red light. I wound down my window and felt the crisp air through my hair and the sun on my face. I felt the smooth wheel glide beneath my hands as I turned the corners. I tuned into the sounds of my favourite song playing, or my kids laughing in the back.

I got to my destination at the same time as the first scenario (maybe even sooner, as I wasn't stressing and worked out a short cut along the way), and while it was the same drive, it was a totally different experience.

Can you feel the difference between the two? Do you notice that there's no 'me time' required? No babysitters or beauty appointments needed? No extra time or financial investment required?

Have you ever considered that driving the kids to school (or anywhere really) could be a sensual experience? If someone had said that to you before, you might've thought they were crazy. I know I would have.

A sensuality practice can be one of the most simple, divine, enriching and rewarding practices for deepening your connection to your body. And there's bonus points if you can play with this practice in moments of self-care, where you get to be really present and mindful, and can squeeze all the juice out of it.

Ever reached the bottom of your morning cuppa and don't remember drinking it? Realising that you didn't smell, taste or enjoy any of it? Well, sensuality is basically the opposite of that.

Heightening our senses in every moment—especially the nourishing, enjoyable, pleasurable moments that we miss when we're in our heads, thinking about the past or the future—helps to bring us back to the now. And helps us experience the pleasures available to us in each moment.

Activity
Make it sensual

A simple, impactful sensuality practice I invite you to begin is simply the act of welcoming sensory input. Bring your awareness to your senses and notice the information you receive in this moment from what you hear, see, smell, taste and touch. Then observe the feedback that arises from your body. Is it good? Or not? Something you like, or not?

Do this in the moment, repetitively, and if you have any aha moments or notice anything interesting that comes up, take it to your journal for expressing.

It is revolutionary—it changes your whole life. If you're going to take one practice away from this book, let it be this one.

Some ideas:

When the babes wake up in the morning

Can you take a moment to snuggle your kids in the morning, feel their warmth and the softness of the back of their neck? Notice the new curl that's twirled itself, smell their little head?

A MOTHER'S PLEASURE

When you're in the kitchen

When you're packing lunch boxes or making a meal, get all cliché and smell the spices, taste the ingredients, move your body to a pleasurable playlist, light a candle, sip a wine (or juice or tea) and actually taste it. (I call this Sensual Sandwiches.)

You're already in the kitchen—you may as well put on some music to fill the room.

You're already handling produce—you may as well feel it.

You're already bringing flavours together—you may as well smell them and taste them.

You're already alive, you may as well be here, now. And you may as well make it sensual.

The feminine deserves reverence and celebration. The feminine is the energy that brings life to the earth.

Chapter five
THE ART OF SENSUALITY

When my second son was two months old, and I was practising sensuality as a mother, I started my business. I couldn't not share what I was discovering and help people that I knew I could. I'd managed to have such a smooth experience in pregnancy and postpartum up until that stage, and felt called to share what I had learned, experienced and put into place to prevent postnatal depression and anxiety, and insomnia.

While I was in a much better state this time around, I didn't want to overcommit and deplete myself through work, so I made a commitment to myself that I was not willing to do anything I didn't want to. I was not willing to 'hustle and grind', or ignore my body's messages and my energy levels. I would only do the things that brought me pleasure—that sparked desire and energised me, rather than depleting me.

And yes, it is possible to run a successful business in this way. I committed to playing, experimenting, being driven by my desires and consciously making it sensual.

An evening to myself for work became a date with my business by candlelight, with soft fabrics to sink into, beautiful stationery with which to explore my ideas, the smell of tea brewing—a warm cup in my hands with my favourite tunes or binaural beats in the background.

Through sensuality, I was creating the ideal environment and energetic state for light-bulb moments, new approaches and opportunities to drop in. It all began to feel so magic and the shift in creativity and abundance was immediate.

I continued to explore and play in my business like this throughout my pregnancy with my third baby, my daughter; what I hadn't expected was for these practices to form the ingredients for an ecstatic birth experience.

The sensual self

By the late stages of my third pregnancy, I realised I hadn't listened to the hypnobirthing tracks I'd planned on listening to, nor read the birthing books I'd planned to read. I missed the prenatal yoga course I had wanted to attend. But streaming sensuality through my life contributed to the most incredible birthing experience, and the most incredible birth imprint my daughter could have.

I birthed her at home in the water under fairy lights, surrounded by my husband and two boys. There was no pain, no fear, no tension. After I pulled my daughter out of the water and onto my chest, I knew I had created deep trust and connection with my body and my intuition. I could now surrender, receive, and connect with my inner knowing—instead of constantly seeking external guidance and validation.

Being connected to your sensual self means connecting to both your body and the present moment—it's a recipe for deep connection and intimacy, whether it be with a child, a partner, or simply with the moment itself.

Sensuality invites you to consistently assess and redefine your desires. It attunes you with what it is that you like—what feels good, what tastes good, what sounds good, what smells good, what looks good to you.

Our senses intensify the way we experience the world. Sensuality brings us home to ourselves. Pleasure reminds us that we are made of a divine magnificence that is available to us in every moment of every day.

In the next chapter we will dive into redefining your desires even further.

The need to nurture

If you have spent many years with your partner and then some being a mother, chances are that you are really good at knowing what those you love enjoy, and you probably often make compromises to prioritise their preferences over your own.

I don't eat meat. I don't like the smell, the taste, the way it looks, the way it feels in my mouth. It grosses me out. But my husband loves lamb. So you know what a special meal at our house often is? Lamb roast. And I'll feed myself a plate of roasted veggies (including three quarters of the tray of roasted potatoes because #potatoesarelife).

The feminine is so devoted to those she loves. So willing to please and nurture and nourish. So resourceful and accommodating when she is resourced. Ultimately, all she needs is to be loved and she will serve those she loves.

The problem arises when she sacrifices too much and loses focus of herself along the way … when weeks, months and years go by and she hasn't directed her life from the point of her own compass in so long that she no longer knows how.

We're going to start now: we're going to indulge ourselves by indulging our senses.

Activity
A sensual feast

This practice is all about summoning your sensuality. Attuning your senses. Calling them in. Turning them up. And fostering a strong and decadent relationship with your body, and your sensuality, that will bring you home to yourself.

It's probably best to plan this one ahead.

A MOTHER'S PLEASURE

Step one

Book in one to two hours to yourself where you won't be interrupted, whether that be in your bedroom one evening, when the kids are at school, or whenever your bestie or family offer to babysit next.

Step two

You're going to create a sensual grazing table for yourself. Gather and invite in as many things as you can that will draw you into a rich sensory experience. Anything that:

- you enjoy eating and drinking—maybe it's chocolate, olives, fruit, champagne, a cup of creamy cacao
- would stimulate the olfactory receptors (smell)—scents, oils or candles
- will create a felt sensation—massage, brushing your hair, using a crystal roller or gua sha tool over the face, moving your body, dancing
- you like to listen to—play music that you can move your body to depending on your energy (ideally something that helps you 'get into your body')
- brings you pleasure to look at—your favourite flowers, candles, a beautified nook in your room

Step three

Spend the next hour or two slowly devouring what you have brought to your sensual grazing table and weaving in different elements, one at a time.

Whilst this is a sensual practice where you get to amplify your senses and practise leading with desire, it is also a practice of awareness, acknowledgement and acceptance. Bring curiosity to the table, and leave any judgement behind.

I invite you to make each choice based on desire—what to taste, what to listen to, how to move, where to touch and massage. It's a practice to be led by you, for you.

Take your time. When it comes to sensuality and pleasure (and most things in life), we tend to rush to the outcome; race to complete the goal. Notice if you do, and ask yourself why. Meet your answers with curiosity and non-judgement.

When you choose to taste something, let it be desire that guides you. Notice if you reach for the healthiest thing first. If choosing some sound or music, notice how you decide on what you want. Enliven all of the senses.

Perhaps you start with a tea or cup of cacao—feel the warmth of it in your hands, smell the aroma, feel your breath as you go to take a sip. Can you see your reflection in the cup? What can you hear as you sip? Savour the flavour.

Here are some elements that you might like to bring to your sensual feast.

Taste	Touch
Sweet	Rose petals
Juicy	Self-massage
Savoury	Oil rub
Spicy	Hair brushing
Indulgent	Food as you savour it
Hot or Cold	Face roller or gua sha tool
Smell	**Sight**
Scented candles	Mirror
Flowers	Candles
Incense	Favourite items
Essential oils	Flowers
Food	Art
Drink	Notice your enviroment

Sound
Music
Binaural beats
Singing bowls
Instrumental music
Dance music
Nature sounds

I hope that now you are starting to realise there are opportunities for every experience to become a sensual one, simply by accessing and tuning into your senses.

Where there is availability for sensuality, there is possibility for pleasure. And if there is the potential for every moment to be a sensual one, there is potential for every moment to be a pleasurable one.

So I guess the question is, can you make it sensual?

Sensuality invites you to consistently assess and redefine your desires.

Chapter six
REDEFINE DESIRE

Desire is the natural gravitational pull that draws the feminine forward. It is the north star to her aligned essence and her truth. It is the thing that shepherds her and her family to more of what they came here for. When she allows herself and is supported to lead herself and her family in the path of her desires, she will direct them along a path of her purpose and pleasure, whether consciously or not.

Sometimes this desire is a craving for sexual expression and intimacy; other times we desire days in bed, curled up with our baby, with no one else touching us. And yet I so often hear from mothers that they feel like they have no desire because they don't want to jump their partner's bones.

There *is* desire—it just may have taken on a different

form. It is still the natural pull forward along the path of purpose and pleasure. However, if it's not a sexual or ambitious desire, mothers can feel like it's not valid. That it's unworthy or insignificant, based on societal ideals and expectations.

Here we get to take a look at what we actually desire, redefine what it means for us now (in comparison to our past selves or society's expectations), and explore ways to activate life force and sexual desire—should that be what we crave.

Let desire be your guide

Have you ever allowed your partner to make a final decision that goes against your desires, thinking they might know better, and when it didn't work out thought, *I knew this would happen!* And then proceeded to get annoyed about the situation (as a reflection of the frustration towards yourself), because you KNEW! If you'd done it the way you wanted, it would've worked out.

I invite you to see your desires as divine guidance; when we have the resources and opportunities to follow our desires, the puzzle pieces of life tend to slot in together easily. Opportunities arise, short cuts are revealed, and life runs a little (or a lot) smoother.

But we must be attuned to and value our desires in order to honour them in the first place.

Distinguishing desire and pleasure

In this chapter, we begin the task of learning about our desires; we will learn to honour them and then get to bear witness to what unfolds in our favour, for ourselves and our family, as a result.

In the previous chapter, we began summoning our sensuality, tuning into our senses, letting our desire guide us in exploring with our senses. This chapter, we go bigger. We get really clear about all of our desires, understand why we might not be feeling sexual desire, and give ourselves the grace and opportunity to redefine what desire is for us.

When we fall in love, we feel loved, alive and happy not just in relation to the person; our entire life reflects love and becomes brighter, more alive. Similarly, when we explore, follow and honour our desires, our pleasure isn't just maximised in relation to the things we desired, but streams through into all areas of our life.

But first, just a reminder of the difference between desire and pleasure. Desire is the thing that you want, while pleasure is an experience that you have, often in relation to the thing that you want, but not necessarily.

For an example, you could say that if cake is what you desire, the experience you have when eating the cake is pleasure.

A process of elimination

In this chapter, we also look at how becoming a mother (and often going through other big transitions or life-changing events) brings the opportunity of consciously choosing our cake (and eating it too).

You may have spent a long time making and eating the same cake, but I wonder how often you consider *Is the cake that I am eating, even the cake that I am enjoying?*

Now's our chance.

- What are some of the things that you know for sure you *don't* want in your life now?
- What in your life does not feel aligned for you right now?

We start with these questions, because sometimes, when we aren't practiced at exploring or even considering what it is we want, it can be easier to determine what it is that we *don't* want, and go from there.

I find in my work that it's common for women to be really unsure about what they want. Chances are they've spent years, if not their entire lives, ignoring what it is that they actually want, and going about achieving the things that they 'should' want instead.

Does it feel easier to compile a list of what you 'should' want instead of what you *do* want?

When desires are discarded

Before we can 'Receive like a goddess' later in the book, we first need to know what it is that we desire.

When we shush, quell or completely ignore our desires

time and time again, we impair our ability to consciously 'clock' our desires; it's like we slowly obscure the communication pathways from our body to our brain that enable us to see, feel and know what it is we actually desire.

Because the thing is, you don't choose your desires; you discover them.

Our body is where our desires usually first present themselves (sometimes it's in our imagination). As a want. A craving. A feeling. Some feelings in relation to desire have been villainised—think about jealousy, envy, greed, lust … probably not things you would feel proud to share. So on top of being conditioned to put our desires last (or ignore them altogether if they aren't socially acceptable), if our desires evoke feelings that aren't socially acceptable, we will ignore, deflect, suppress and abandon them further, continuing to interrupt that connection with our body and her messages for us.

This is one of the many reasons why kids are so damn awesome. They haven't been conditioned to not want what they want. They are clear about what they want. They're not afraid to acknowledge what they want and take action to get it. There is a defined, clear connect between their desires revealing themselves and the pathway to their pleasures; this allows them to be aware of, acknowledge and express their heart's desires (and is incredibly useful when it comes to weaving more pleasure into our lives).

So what is it that separates us as mothers from our childhood selves, who were likely very clear about their desires?

Some of these might feel true for you.

- Societal, cultural, historical and familial conditioning
- A lifetime spent learning to be the 'giver' and performing to keep others comfortable
- Not feeling worthy, allowed, deserving or entitled
- Feeling desperate to please
- Associating giving pleasure with being of value (as opposed to receiving)
- Associate receiving with being frivolous, transactional, selfish and shameful
- The desire to be The Good Mother outweighs all other desires. (My hot tip—I've had my time being The Good Mother … it wasn't that fun.)

Is there anything else that you can add to this list?

If we aren't sure what it is we want when it comes to pleasure (or anything), how can we seek it, be open to it, invoke it and ultimately receive it?

The creative catalyst

The divine design of the feminine is to receive; anatomically, emotionally and energetically. She is also a powerful creator, most effective when driven by desire—not driven by goals, accountability or willpower. These are more masculine attributes that require a lot of energy. When you rely solely on creating anything from willpower, force, accountability, grit or 'manning up', you will find yourself

A MOTHER'S PLEASURE

in an energy slump, potentially unable to finish the thing that you started. Perhaps this is why nature forces us into our feminine in pregnancy. To be skilled and practiced at creating in a sustainable way that doesn't burn us out.

Our desires lead us to create what we are here to create—whether that be a baby, an outfit, a meal, an offering, an adventure, an event, an artwork or a community—and through the materialisation of our desires, we can experience pleasure.

Consider the most recent times in your life when you've felt a lack of desire to create—not just art, but anything. Chances are you were feeling low in energy, perhaps low emotionally; maybe not deep depression, but just a lack of lust for life.

When you don't have much desire or inspiration to create anything, it makes everything a little more grey, more boring, more 'just going through the motions', whether it be creating a plan for the day, an outfit to wear, a meal, an adventure with the kids, or a new project for work.

When we lack desire, we are lacking creative energy or life-force energy, which is also sexual energy. When we lack this life-force energy, everything is a lot less colourful, and a lot less pleasurable. We put on whatever clothes are clean or comfortable instead of creating an outfit that expresses our essence. We throw a thoughtless dinner on the table instead of creating a meal. We put ourselves in close proximity to our loved ones, but aren't present to create deep connection, trust or intimacy. We 'go through the motions' of sex without creating intimacy, arousal or ecstasy.

Do any of these behaviours resonate? Is there anywhere in your life where you feel like you're simply going through the motions, without any desire or inspiration?

Liberating desire

We now know that we don't choose our desires; our desires reveal themselves. And following our desires allows us to create pleasure in our lives.

But what if our desires aren't revealing themselves to us? What if we don't feel desire in order to follow its direction toward pleasure?

This is something I deeply craved the answers to, especially coming out of my postnatal mental health struggles. Not only did I hope to feel into all parts of life again; I wanted to feel *the desire* to feel into all parts of life again, you know? I didn't just want to spark creativity in life again; I wanted to feel desire for that first.

What I discovered was that when I was nourished, nurtured and supported enough to fill my 'basic needs cup', it then overflowed into my 'life-force energy cup', which is also responsible for sexual energy. It's the one that informs our desire.

It makes sense that we need to be full in our basic needs cup first before we can create (a baby or anything else).

Here we'll begin to explore how to fill our basic needs cup so that it flows into our life-force energy cup—igniting desire and creating more pleasure.

This will also be helpful in nourishing our nervous

system. With our mental load at an all-time high, most of us mothers are moving through our days fuelled by coffee and adrenaline; we're constantly stimulating our sympathetic (fight or flight) nervous system, putting us in a survival state where what might've previously turned us on now feels like a threat. This is one of the reasons why the idea of sex with our partner might feel like an attack, even if we know it will be good for us, or it's something we want to want.

When we can drop into the parasympathetic nervous system and land in our bodies, advances from our partner (or, more broadly, from opportunities in life) might go from repulsive and jarring to something that we start to turn towards, or something that we desire and initiate.

Even if our desire doesn't spontaneously switch itself 'on', we will notice that it becomes more responsive to life.

The basic needs cup

If you identify as a feminine being at the core, and you've been doing ALL the things, then you've likely been moving with masculine energy, of which feminine beings have a finite amount. Therefore you've been unknowingly creating energy leaks and depleting your basic needs cup, and there's no overflow into your life-force cup.

If you aren't feeling desire at the moment, even for the things that you used to, I invite you to consider and explore the levels of your basic needs cup, and how your nervous system is functioning.

And if you feel depleted and 'burnt out', we will explore how to fill this energetic cup and seal some of the leaks so that we can:

- allow desire to reveal itself
- increase the flow of desire
- spark creative and life-force energy
- experience more pleasure

When trying to fill the basic needs cup with things that used to feel good and nurture us, if we aren't conscious, we can end up spending our time, space, energy and money on activities, outings, people, rituals and appointments that now leave us feeling unfulfilled, bored and a little bit depressed. This is likely because we thought we 'should', because those things used to feel pleasurable to us, because we've lost our connection with our desire.

If this resonates with you, know that there's nothing wrong with you. Perhaps you're in the gap between where your desires once were and where they are now, or perhaps it's a marker that will help you realise your cup is no longer overflowing. Know that this is one of the greatest things about becoming a mama. A beautiful opportunity has been brought to your attention—one that you can now explore for deeper enrichment of your life and relationships.

A process of discovery

Before I became a mother, I thought I was well equipped to nurture myself, fill my cup, and ensure I felt resourced. I had a great collection of self-care practices for when my baby arrived.

There were a few problems with this situation though. The first was that I was policing myself in an attempt to be the perfect mother; this meant prioritising everything else over the things that filled my basic needs cup, which prevented overflow into my life-force energy cup. What I also hadn't taken into account was that many of the things that had created overflow previously didn't fit easily into the throes of early motherhood. And even the ones that did no longer felt all that fulfilling.

My wants had kind of changed. I'd gone through such a big transition (and an ego death) and was in a place where I had the opportunity to redefine my desires. I witness this in my work when clients are doing all of the things they think they 'should' do, and all of the things they used to enjoy, and are often left feeling unfulfilled—like the time that they were finally able to use to create some overflow for themselves was 'wasted' on things that just felt like another tick off the to-do list.

When we move through matrescence, the process from maiden to mother, our values shift to include a whole new little person (or persons!) in our life, whom a lot of our energy, time and attention goes to; this makes us more conscious of how we allocate the energy, time and attention we have left. If we have been pregnant, there are bodily changes that happen, as well as the shift in our identity: from who we were to who we are now. Not only has a child been brought into your life, but a new version of you has been brought to life, and this new you has new desires to be discovered. So let's go find them!

First we'll play with a practice that builds strong body-to-brain communication pathways so that we can feel what it is that we do and don't desire. Then we'll spark desire from filling that basic needs cup.

Activity 1
Discerning desire

As often as possible, when making decisions, ask your body yes/no questions about what she wants, and listen to what she has to say, and how she says it. Start with what it is she wants to eat and drink, and then move into other areas of your life.

Offer your body the opportunity to choose and you might be surprised with what she desires.

At breakfast, holding the eggs in your hands, ask her—*Do you want eggs today? No? Peanut butter toast then? Yes!*

Do you want coffee?

Do you feel like taking the kids to the beach today?

Do you want to have a quiet day?

You might find it eye opening to discover that the coffee—or wine or chocolate or whatever it is that you thought you couldn't stop consuming because you liked it so much or thought your body needed it—isn't what your body wants at all.

Note: If a to-do list feels like a 'get to-do' list, you know it is driven by desire.

Activity 2
Igniting desire

Let's create your unique Feel-Good Guide. This will help you explore what it is that creates overflow of your basic needs cup into your life-force cup. We will spark desire to lead us to our pleasure. It means we'll get to know ourselves on a deeper level.

Be open, be curious. Treat this as an exploration of what it is that you truly desire. Not the 'shoulds', not the standard, not the societal norms. Your unique desires.

Simply begin a list of all of the things that feel good for you. Keep adding to it over days and weeks until you have a really comprehensive list to pick and choose from as you please. Every time you are enjoying yourself, notice what it is you're doing, and put it in your Feel-

Good Guide, as well as the things you know feel good. We'll add more to this in the next chapter too.

Be aware of, and record, what is pleasurable for you now, as you move through your days. It's worthwhile to include as many items as you can that can be done with your children or while working, if that's how you spend a lot of your time.

These don't need to be grand activities or adventures; it could be really simple things that take minimal time, where you don't have to leave your home. The more accessible they are to you in whatever season you're in, the better.

While regular bushwalks with your bub in a carrier (for example) are awesome, grounding your bare feet in the earth for your morning coffee or lying on a rug looking up at the sky are things that can be easily woven through your life regularly (and therefore can top up your basic needs cup more regularly).

Let desire be your guide.

Chapter seven
SELF-CARE AND ITS INSUFFICIENCIES

Right now, post-pandemic, when we are further isolated from community and carrying more than we ever have before, the idea that simply doing more self-care activities like getting massages and 'taking fifteen minutes a day for yourself' does little to ease or resolve how a lot of us are feeling.

What do we need to surrender to a more sustainable pace of life? Safety.

What do we need to be, to feel calm? Resourced.

What do we need in order to sink into a level of intimacy? Connection.

We got ninety-nine problems and a list of self-care to-dos is one of them.

You might've noticed there is a lot of messaging shouting 'Self-care! Self-care!' at mothers. Like it's some magic key to living in mamahood bliss.

In reality, it's insufficient and insulting.

The self-care paradox

Chances are you've had your fair share of phases of consuming and following the self-care story. Perhaps you've been left still depleted, or exhausted, with a feeling of failure (for not doing self-care 'right') and a drop, or maybe an overwhelming amount, of guilt (feeling like you shouldn't have spent time on yourself).

For mothers in our society, self-care is like another tightrope we are trying to walk.

We're conditioned to believe that doing anything for ourselves is a luxury, and yet it's also expected that we take the initiative to prioritise self-care. And if we're having a hard time—emotionally, physically or mentally—then we obviously aren't taking enough care of ourselves. This paradoxical expectation doesn't take into account the invisible barriers that prevent a mother from giving herself permission for pleasure, nor does it factor in the weight of carrying what should be a community responsibility on her own.

I see the opportunity for this generation of mothers to undo this societal conditioning within themselves and their households, and eradicate the burden of it entirely for the next generation.

The Mother's Self-Care cocktail served up by our patriarchal society is a mix of:

- responsibility (as community care isn't normalised or often available)
- a splash of ownership (it's on you to be ok)
- a pinch of pressure (to accentuate the aforementioned responsibility and ownership)
- failure for flavour (when we don't get the balancing act 'right')
- a big squeeze of guilt (for the lifetime of socialisation that reminds us we shouldn't need anything for ourselves)

I don't have the answers for creating a supportive community for mothers, but what we can do to change the culture is work within ourselves.

The value of pleasure

Here's what I know for sure.
    Pleasure makes the heavy, lighter.
    It makes the dark, brighter.
    It makes the monotonous, enjoyable.
    It makes the boring, desirable.
    And it's not finite: more pleasure for yourself does not equal less pleasure for someone else.
    Pleasure is something we could all use more of right now, to make whatever shitshow we're in a little less shit, or to make the good times even better.

Next we're going to:

- look at why self-care prescription alone doesn't work
- demystify the limitations or obstacles to self-care in our society
- explore ways to make the foundations of self-care not a list but a lifestyle in order to feel fuelled and cup filled—not solely to 'be a better mama', but to have a better life for yourself and your family

The new normal

I hope in years to come, when our children become parents, there will be no need for this chapter. I hope there will be much greater value placed on mothers and therefore greater societal support for them, so they can nurture themselves and the next generation.

I hope that by reading this book and letting go of your self-care 'dilemmas' (which we'll cover further in this chapter), you won't unknowingly pass them on to your children, so they will be free of such burdened conditioning to begin with.

I hope that a mother looking after herself and being looked after by others will be the most natural, assumed way of being, without the feeling it must be earned or fought for, and without overwhelming guilt attached. It will simply be the way it is; the way it was always meant to be.

I hope that taking care of ourselves once we've become

mothers will be considered as necessary as sleeping, using the toilet, eating, and washing ourselves (which, especially in the early mothering years, can often be put on the bottom of the needs list after the needs of others—and even seen as self-care activities instead of the basic needs that they are). I hope that anything that might seem on the more 'decadent' end of the self-care spectrum will be less about special occasions or reviving ourselves from depletion and more about supporting ourselves day to day.

Creating a lifestyle over a list of to-dos

Instead of adding the traditional self-care prescription or to-do list to our already overflowing plate, what if we simply committed to one question, regularly, through whatever it is we're already showing up to? What if we were to ask ourselves on repeat: *How can I make this pleasurable?* Once you start to ask this question on the regular, it will feel less like an exercise in self-indulgence and more like a simple way of lighting up your life and the lives of others.

As the first step, I invite you to start putting your basic needs first:

- Pee when you need to pee
- Drink when you're thirsty
- Eat when you're hungry
- Go to bed when you're tired (when you can)

This was one of the very first things I started with when

I was recovering from postnatal depression, anxiety and insomnia.

If you had told me before becoming a mother that one of my 'self-care' practices was going to be taking myself to the toilet or getting myself a drink when I needed it, I wouldn't have believed you.

Before becoming a mother, I'd spent over a decade practising and teaching yoga and meditation. I had great awareness of my body. I'm an exercise physiologist—I've studied neurology, physiology and biology. I knew about the hormonal changes and physiology of pregnancy and birth, and the neurology of the mama brain. But none of it helped me to maintain my mental and emotional wellbeing.

I'd also worked as a health and wellness coach for years, so I knew the importance of healthy eating and exercise.

But I had a lot more trouble than I expected looking after myself whilst looking after my son, and it got to the point where I was not meeting my most basic of needs; this was where I started my rehabilitation.

Not to say that you need rehabilitating, but chances are, if you've fallen in love with your child and you've just gotten them to sleep (on you, likely), it will be really easy to not question that status quo, and place your needs on the backburner.

A well mother

You might've come across the tongue-in-cheek joke that gets passed around on socials—something along the lines of:

'Sleep when the baby sleeps.'

'Ok sure, and I'll clean when the baby cleans!'

It's popular culture memes and 'jokes' like this that demonstrate our society's lack of value towards mothers and illuminate an undercurrent of cultural expectations, societal norms, and general collective disregard for a mother's wellbeing. It doesn't take long to notice the message everywhere in our society that having a clean home is more important than having a well-rested mother.

We also see it in the way mothers are matter-of-fact about prioritising household chores over time spent with their children, but to prioritise something for themselves over their children in the same way is laced with guilt.

It's possible to get to the point where a mother's satiation of self is just as imperative as having clean dishes to use and clean clothes to wear.

Might we begin to consider the value a well mother has in our society over a clean house? And yet that is one of the yardsticks of being a 'good mother'—being a good housekeeper.

In reality, they are two completely different roles.

Weaving in self-care

Whilst society can seem to encourage mothers to 'Sleep when the baby sleeps,' it's the absence of respect and value for motherhood that modern mums hear the loudest. With minimal support systems and a lack of closely connected community, mothers don't feel resourced enough to factor in self-care, and so it gets pushed to the side. And the idea that time, space and energy are all required for self-care persists.

So instead of the standard lecture on 'Self-care! Self-care!' we will explore some of the barriers to self-care and pleasure, along with some invaluable, practical ways to weave pleasure into your days—with or without your children around. No babysitters required, no extra time, no extra money, no feeling exhausted just from juggling the self-care scheduling amongst everything else. Just the pure and simple receiving of self-care and pleasure that is actually going to fulfil you, feel effortless and become a lifestyle over a list of to-dos.

You'll learn how to weave in self-care when you feel as though you are under-resourced, under-supported and only just keeping your head above water. Chances are you already have a full plate, so me just giving you a list of self-care practices isn't going to work, and here's why: I'm not a gambling woman, but I bet that you're a smart woman, and I bet you already know self-care activities that would be helpful to you right now. So there must be reasons why you are not doing those things. I invite you to consider this and maybe jot down what comes up for you in your journal.

Might I offer you a suggestion? Might it be that there is a multitude of inner beliefs that prevent you from weaving self-care into your life on the regular? And might this be due to past conditioning—what you have previously been told, shown or advised by society, other mothers or your own mother?

Might there be unconscious programming playing out in your mind that you're not aware of? A programming that's ever so subtly preventing you from taking action and actually doing those self-care things? And perhaps you have structured your whole life around those programs or stories without ever reflecting on whether you believe them or not. If you don't believe them, here we'll have the chance to delete them from our programming, and replace them with new programs that contribute to filling our cup to overflow.

We often don't do enough self-care because it is presented in our masculine society as another list of things we have to 'do' and schedule in—another thing that we feel like we 'should' be doing more of, and if we're not, we feel a sense of failure.

What is actually required to shift this thinking is an entire new culture where self-care is not separate from the way we move through life; it shifts from being a thing that needs to be completed, to the way we BE, like a golden thread in the tapestry of our life. It becomes part of your lifestyle once you start to update your past programming.

Just like showering and brushing your teeth, it becomes non-negotiable. It isn't about luxury or having earned it; it's just something that you do.

The barriers

Here's what I've experienced and what I see in the world of mothering and self-care.

Even though we know what's 'good for us'—what makes us feel resourced, energised and fuelled—we often don't do it due to a number of things. So let's begin to explore what can get in the way of us being devoted to self-care, pleasure and the things that bring us enjoyment and fill our cup.

Can you relate to any of these?

- Deeply held cultural beliefs of what a 'good mother' is, and what a 'good mother' does and doesn't do. For example: 'A good mother is with her children twenty-four seven' or 'A good mother puts her children first, always' or 'A good mother has a tidy home.' I think we can agree that these kinds of beliefs are outdated, untrue, and unhelpful in experiencing life through a lens of ecstasy.

- Expectations placed on ourselves by ourselves, based on our pre-mama identity. Perhaps an identity where we were high achievers, productive, independent and the capitalist version of 'successful', which can be really unachievable and unattainable in this whole new construct that is motherhood.

- Society's representation and stereotyping of a good mother through the media

- The Madonna-whore dichotomy that is subtlety infused in patriarchal society, where a mother is perceived as either the pure, chaste, 'good' Madonna mother figure, or the immoral, promiscuous 'bad' whore mother. This social undercurrent acts as a judgemental gatekeeper, often preventing mothers from being open to and claiming their birthright to pleasure, sensuality and sexuality. We break down this dichotomy by merging the two as we continue to express our full-spectrum selves as mothers.

- The Martyr Mother: Unconsciously believing that we must sacrifice the things that matter to us most in order to participate in self-care, let alone self-pleasure.

- An overwhelming sense of guilt, selfishness or shame when we do go ahead and take part in self-care. This can lead to choosing something that society views as productive over pleasurable, or opting out of self-care altogether due to the discomfort.

- We unconsciously default to prioritising our time according to what our culture deems important or expected of a mother, leaving minimal time available for enjoyment or pleasure.

- Not knowing what would even feel good or fill your cup any more. (Hopefully we covered that in 'Redefine desire'.)

The good news is that, when you begin to make the unconscious conscious, and peel back some of the layers that hold you from self-care as a way of life, you can start to understand what is creating friction. You can begin to identify where the resistance is coming from, neutralise it, let go of it and create new narratives that align with you leading a fuelled, pleasure-full life. It will make participation in self-care practices not just something that you do now and then, but a lifestyle.

Loving ourselves

In this chapter we will begin to dismantle the common self-care dilemmas that mothers face, and later in the book, you will learn how following desires that direct you to pleasure is not simply self-care, but a tool for self-discovery and personal growth, helping you return home to your whole, satiated self.

On one hand, I want to help you to do all of the self-care things, and on the other hand I want to throw the term in the bin completely and say that these things should just be ways of life. My stance on self-care is that it's really important for a mother to do things that nourish her body, mind and soul, but simply telling a mother to 'do more self-care' ignores the reality that prevents her from doing so in the first place. I'm not talking about barriers of time, energy or money—I'm talking about the way she feels about herself, her feelings of not having earned the self-care, the sense that there are always more 'important' things to do than be kind, gentle and loving towards herself, because this is what she's been taught over her lifetime.

So here's what we'll do—we'll begin with some really simple ways to uncover our relationship to loving ourselves. I'll use the term self-care, and we'll explore and unravel hopefully most—if not all—of the things that are preventing you from moving from the old paradigm of a self-care to-do list that is rarely visited, to a place where loving yourself is a lifestyle.

This is also a good practice for fostering a great relationship with your body, where pleasure lies. Many women find that they are quite disconnected from their bodies, which means they're disconnected from pleasure (as we know from our 'Summoning your sensuality' chapter). So know that as you start to listen for your body's messages, you will have the opportunity to honour those messages, which builds that connection with your body and allows you to further practise meeting your needs and desires.

Demonstrate your worth, know your value

When we honour our needs and desires, it demonstrates to the world the standard at which we are to be treated. It shows our children what to expect should they become mothers, fathers, partners, friends and community members.

When we begin to put self-pleasure over the dishes, it sets an example for those we live with.

When we honour our boundaries and say no to someone, we show them how boundaries can be respected.

When we step aside and leave the things that we thought we had to do, it gives others the opportunity to step up, and provides us with evidence that we are supported.

Now we have gotten familiar with some of the 'whys', in the next chapters we will look at the how; let me just tell you it's going to change your life, improve your relationships and the energy in your household, and loosen those tight binds of societal suppression not just for yourself but for society as a whole—hello culture change!

Here are your practices for this chapter:

Activity 1
Honour your needs

Listen to and honour your basic needs immediately (e.g. pee when you need to pee).

Note: your needs are NEEDS, not pleasures.

We start here at ground zero, learning how to honour our basic needs, before moving on to removing obstacles to our pleasures.

Notice any resistance that comes up in your mind and jot it down. Not for the purpose of judgement, but for the purpose of knowing what programs are installed so that you can delete, update, reprogram and upgrade if you desire. (e.g. *All the children need to be fed first before I can sit down to eat.*) Notice it, jot it down and see it as an interesting idea—we'll explore how we can untangle and remove it as an obstacle in the next chapter.

Activity 2
Add to your Feel-Good Guide

Remember to add to your Feel-Good Guide. What things that feel like self-pleasure are available to you? Perhaps without requiring a babysitter, more money or time, a clean house first, etc.

Here are some experiences that nourish the feminine to get you started:

Nurture in nature:
- Ocean swims
- Nature walks
- Hot cuppas in the sun

Music and movement:
- Pram or baby carrier walk while listening to an audiobook, music or a podcast
- Moving your body in any way that feels good

Connection and friendship:
- Going grocery shopping or to the markets with friends
- Cooking or doing chores with friends
- Attending a women's circle

Nourishment and body care:
- Fresh sheets

- Face masks
- A warming bev after a long night comforting your littlies

Pleasure makes the heavy, lighter.
It makes the dark, brighter.
It makes the monotonous, enjoyable.
It makes the boring, desirable.

Chapter eight
RECEIVE LIKE A GODDESS

Recently on my way home from a morning walk, I stopped at my favourite little coffee shop and sat down for a quick coffee in the sun before the day ramped up.

(One gift of becoming a mother is that a tiny pocket of time filled with peace, quiet and personal space can feel like an expanse of time that I might have previously taken for granted!)

I was feeling generous and loved up and ordered hubs his extra-hot flat white to walk home to him. As the barista handed it to me, he asked, 'Do you want me to double up the cup for you?'

I said, 'Yes please, that'd be great.'

So off home I went, only to realise that perhaps a year or even six months ago I would've said, 'Oh no, it's *fiiiine*. I'm all good,' and proceeded to spend the entire ten-minute walk home juggling the burning-hot coffee from one hand to the other as the flesh from my palms melted onto the footpath.

It got me thinking. Why would I have denied the barista's double cup offer before?

Because I didn't want to inconvenience him.

Because I could 'cope' without the second cup.

Because I didn't want to make a fuss.

Because the feminist in me said I can look after myself.

Because the people-pleasing tendencies we inherit as females go deep.

Because the programming we swallow down, switch on and continue to play out as a mother says, *I am the one who looks after others, not the one to be looked after.*

Because it was an unconscious default setting to say 'No thanks' to receiving, until it wasn't.

These are some of the many reasons why we as women, in motherhood, have such a hard time receiving pleasure—pleasure in the bedroom, pleasure with our children, pleasure in the housekeeping, pleasure for pleasure's sake.

Might I now remind you that we are miraculous human beings, here on Earth for a divine experience filled with pleasure.

Say yes to receiving

Over the next two chapters, we will learn to make friends with our desires, say yes to receiving, and enjoy receiving what we desire without insurmountable guilt and shame.

A MOTHER'S PLEASURE

The thing is, the way we receive one thing is the way we receive everything.

I invite you to think about it—how do you receive?

How do you receive compliments, offers of help, gifts, affection, pleasure, a double coffee cup so you don't lose a hand?

Chances are you've been taught in some form or another that receiving is not for you. Do any of these feel familiar?

Receiving is transactional (to receive, you must give something in return).

Receiving help means you're not coping.

Receiving a compliment means you're not humble.

Receiving affection means you must give it back.

Our ability (or inability) to receive pleasure is the measure of our internalised societal value and self-worth. Our society does not value a mother's work and therefore the level of pleasure we're willing to receive is minimal. We must be productive (or even suffer) before we are 'deserving' of receiving and experiencing pleasure—a hot cup of tea, a few moments in the sun doing nothing, reading, a nap time of self or partnered pleasure.

When you begin to open to receiving, you'll notice you actually open the floodgates to greater abundance. You'll open yourself to more help, more support, more money, more time, space, energy—EVERYTHING! And you get to choose to say, *Yes, and more please.*

The barriers to receiving

At my mother blessing for my third baby, one of my best friends confessed that she wished she'd done more for me after my first son was born, during my journey through postnatal depression, anxiety and insomnia. I thought back to that time and I remembered how forgotten I'd felt. How much I wanted someone to take the reins of caring for me, even if just for ten minutes—to make me a cup of tea and run a bath. How I had fantasised about meals left on the doorstep that never came. How I had expected it to be different, expected to have felt more 'held' and received more help.

I realised in that moment, under the trees in the dappled sunshine by the rolling waves, 'I'm not sure I would have been able to receive it.'

Energetically, I had created a boundary to receiving because of all that I had internalised, believed and integrated as part of my identity.

Before becoming a mother, I had spent my entire life proving to the world (and myself) that I was independent, that I was capable, that I could achieve anything I set my mind to. I didn't need help to do anything, and I'd assumed that would continue after becoming a mother.

I believe part of the reason I experienced postnatal depression and anxiety seven months into motherhood was because of all the white knuckling I was doing trying to maintain the independence that was such a big part of my identity. We know it takes a village to raise a child, but what I discovered was that even if there had been the traditional village available to me to help raise my child, at that point on my journey, I don't think I would've accepted the help.

There were more conversations made around the help I wanted to receive with each subsequent pregnancy and birth, but I couldn't have those conversations until I became conscious of the barriers within that prevented me from receiving. Ultimately, I couldn't get to a place of being supported until I was able to open myself to receiving support.

Creating new truths

As I became aware of narratives that held me back from receiving, I slowly began replacing them with narratives that opened me up to receiving, and therefore changed my relationship to receiving.

The old truths
- Asking for or accepting help means I'm weak or not coping
- I shouldn't need anyone else to help with housekeeping
- Receiving affection or pleasure from my husband means I have to 'put out' and pay it back
- People only give me compliments to be nice

My new truths
- Asking for or accepting help is a gift to the person who wants to give

- Sharing a house with my husband means shared housekeeping responsibilities
- I can receive pleasure and affection for pleasure's sake
- Receiving compliments gracefully means giving someone an opportunity to give

This new connection between the way I felt about receiving and what I actually received, and the processes of getting from one to the other—along with years of inner work, work with clients and studies of quantum physics—meant that by my third pregnancy I knew I could choose how this experience was going to go for me.

Activity
Reframe your receiving reflex

Become aware of your relationship to receiving by noticing the moments of your day where there is opportunity to receive anything, and observe your thoughts, feelings and stories that arise.

1. Become aware: notice the opportunity to receive.
2. Observe: notice your reaction and default

response to what you're being offered. What feels ok to receive? What doesn't?
3. Acknowledge: notice what you say no to, ask yourself why and jot it all down in your journal. What's the story?
4. Reframe: what's a more helpful meaning or thought? Change the story and continue to remind yourself of that whenever the opportunity arises.

And to take this even further:

5. Level up: your challenge now is to say yes (or the appropriate version of yes) to every opportunity you desire to receive. Notice what comes up for you.
6. Express discomfort: chances are you feel really uncomfortable. Consider how you can express that discomfort from your body in a healthy way whilst being in the energy of receiving. Some ways to express discomfort include journalling, movement or dancing, talking with a friend or mentor, through art or other creative pursuits whilst still having said yes to receiving. We explore expression in greater detail in the chapter 'Pleasure pathways'.
7. Practise: Keep flexing your receiving muscle until one day when you say yes to a second coffee cup you blow your mind at how far you've come.

The ripple effect of receiving

The societal conditioning we've all been immersed in when it comes to the role of a mother and a mother's needs and wants has not only done a massive disservice to us as mothers—potentially leaving us feeling depressed, depleted and defeated; it's also done a massive disservice to our partnerships, our parenting and the families in our society.

It's not only us who miss out when we don't allow ourselves to receive like a goddess. When we say yes to receiving, we say yes to being better resourced and having a heightened mood and higher perspective. We can be present and respond in a steady, regulated way instead of react in a reflexive and potentially damaging way, which means we can deepen our intimate connections with self, with life, with our children and our partners.

Your pleasure is yours

I often get asked, 'How do I explain to my partner the benefits of me prioritising "me time", self-care and pleasure so that I can devote myself to this family? Feel better in myself? Not feel so stretched? How do I get them to step up and support me to do this?' Or some version of that.

When you have uncovered what it is you'd like to receive, opened to it, and then built up the courage to ask for it and not been understood, valued or met, it can be really defeating and bring up feelings of resentment and frustration. It might stop us from ever asking again.

We've ALL been socialised to believe that mothers are to do the majority of the caring, housekeeping, organising and such. Fathers have not been immune to this messaging, this modelling, this conditioning, which means they're often not aware of how to better be of service, of what it is we are carrying, of how we feel in carrying this load.

What ends up happening is that we lean further into our masculine energy, which, by virtue of the universal law of polarity, pushes our partners into their feminine. This means we are in the driver's seat (being goal oriented and driven to do all of the things), and our partners are pushed into surrender, into being, into softening—not the energy that is going to whisk us off our feet, be our knights in shining armour and do all the things that are wearing us down.

When we prioritise our pleasure, it moves us out of our masculine, and allows our partners to move into their masculine. This means we energetically and metaphorically step aside, so that they can step up. No conversation, argument or asking required—put the scrubbing brush down and walk away; now's the perfect time for self-pleasure.

Traditionally we might think we need to tell, teach or demand what we want of anyone, especially our partners. However, when we do this, it puts them in the place of possession. Our partners do not possess our pleasure; we do. And it is our responsibility to seek, find and experience it—for ourselves, for our partnerships, for our relationships with our children and for the sake of pleasure itself.

We are not our household's employee, nor is our partner our boss. We do not require their permission to seduce ourselves with the sensualities of life. We do not need to give them a list of the benefits of our self-care. We do not need to explain how much better we feel when our cup is full. We do not need to tell them how important it is for the children to have a mother who feels good. We don't have to say a word: we simply need to BE it, and they will FEEL it.

They will feel your lightness, they will feel the tension dissipate, they will feel your yes, your openness. They will notice that easy-breezy you, because they will feel it through them.

And to them? It feels good. It is what every partner craves—the fullness of the goddess, the satiated woman, the fulfilled woman who can surrender to life like a gentle stream into the ocean.

She'll be noticed, she'll be felt, and she'll be revered as much as she reveres herself, for she is magnificent and she resides in ALL of us.

So if you feel yourself saying *I'm ready to receive but they aren't giving!* or *I want to receive but I'm sick of just waiting for it to happen* or *How can I get them to understand the benefits of self-care or 'me time'?* then try this:

1. Ask yourself what you want them to give you
2. Now give that to yourself

Show, don't tell

I invite you to ask yourself the question, *How can I show, rather than tell? How can I show my partner what it is I desire, in a way they will witness, feel and notice?*

It might take some time, or no time at all, but it is more effective than any kind of telling or teaching. It also won't feel like parenting your partner or trying to tell them what to do.

When I began my business, I'd get really frustrated with my husband for not 'supporting me' by giving me time for my work. Instead of trying to explain to him the benefits of me spending time in my business, I showed him those benefits by protecting the time I'd set aside to work, actually taking that time for work, and coming back as an energised, upbeat, happier version of myself.

What I desire finds me

Prioritising our pleasure, being self-focussed and caring for ourselves through pure enjoyment are divine acts of devotion that empower our partner to witness the goddess that's living alongside them and offers them an opportunity to honour her appropriately.

When we've spent most of our lives being encouraged to achieve, go after what we want, take the steps and make the moves, one of the most powerful moves we can make is to surrender. To be open. To call in what we'd like to receive as opposed to seeking it out. Receiving is a feminine art form that is perceived as passive, but in reality is energetically active.

We can actively open ourselves to receiving by surrendering the doing of all the things. By taking the importance out of what 'needs to get done' and placing it instead on what would feel fun; what would nourish; what would soothe; what would bring satisfaction, enjoyment or pleasure.

My friend Callie Brown said once, 'What I desire finds me,' and this is exactly the energy you get to learn here. And when you've mastered it, you get to receive like the goddess that you are.

So what do you desire?

I'd desired and then declared that my third baby would bring abundance. I programmed in a new belief that I am always supported, because if I was going to be welcoming in abundance, this would also mean abundance of support—logistically, physically, emotionally and mentally.

After having my babe, it was really easy to run client sessions at first because she would just be sleeping by my side or on the boob. This worked until a few months in when she was awake a lot more and wouldn't always settle with a boob or a snuggle.

I could have done what I would have done a few years back: cut some of my sessions, schedule and strategise, believing I had to sacrifice one or the other (my work or my family). But instead, for the next month or two, I trusted that I would receive the support I needed. I focussed on being open to receiving in whatever form it came and practising gratitude when it arrived. I focussed on surrendering. On stepping aside so that someone or something else could step up. On reminding myself that not only was I always supported, but I was more supported than ever.

And what happened after that was pretty entertaining—every client session already booked in over the next three months that wasn't covered by Jake being home to care for our daughter was taken care of in one way or another. Whether my daughter had an unusually long nap, Jake had an unexpected early finish from work, or someone rescheduled to a time when I had care—it worked out every single time.

Goddess energy

I realise that I'm asking a lot of you—I'm asking you to trust. To surrender. And I know that perhaps that hasn't felt safe for you before. Or perhaps you haven't had much practice at it.

The good news is this: it happens really quickly. The dishes that you decide to step away from are washed by the next evening. The meeting that you prioritised pleasure over gets rescheduled. The birthday present for which you missed the cut-off delivery date you find in the window of a store you walk past. This is not about playing some kind of domestic duty cat-and-mouse; it's about you being devoted to yourself, shifting your energy to that of the goddess and life getting the memo and obliging.

It might actually astound you how effective it is to play with your mind and energy like this, and see results almost immediately. And if you don't, keep opening, keep trusting. Try not to become contracted, impatient and tense … remember we want to receive pleasure, and the way we receive pleasure is the same way we receive anything: by believing we are worthy.

You are a miraculous
human being,
here on Earth for a
divine experience
filled with pleasure.

Chapter nine
PLEASURE AS A TOOL FOR SELF-DISCOVERY AND LIBERATION

After giving birth to baby number two, I discovered that most of what I believed to be true and right when it came to being a mother and experiencing pleasure was nothing more than a collection of ideas, comments, stories and experiences that I had been told or received through the media and indirect messaging, or that had been modelled to me. I had taken on these stories as truth and integrated them into my body and my psyche, with this process starting as far back as childhood.

I had been holding on to that collection of ideas, believing them to be true, and had unknowingly used them to scaffold my entire existence as a mother.

In his book *Breaking the Habit of Being Yourself*, Dr Joe Dispenza says that by the time we are thirty-five years old, ninety-five per cent of our life is run by a subconscious program that creates our entire reality. Our behaviours, attitudes, beliefs, habits and skills are governed by this program, which means we'll continue to think, feel and react in the same ways day to day, year to year. (We might, for example, automatically turn to food when we're upset, or say yes to every little thing people ask of us.)

We are set to continue with this curated program until we make the unconscious conscious. One way of doing this (the most pleasurable way) is by following our desires, and using pleasure as a tool, as a magnifying glass, to bring those behaviours, attitudes, beliefs, emotional reactions, habits, skills, associative memories, conditioned responses and perceptions to the surface, so that we can decide if they're the scaffolding we want to shape our reality. If not, we can choose what we'd prefer instead.

If you've done any kind of personal development work before, chances are you've done some journalling, talk therapy, meditation, dreaming or visioning, and I'm guessing you probably didn't know that you could use pleasure as a tool. I'm also guessing that, as you are here reading this, you're up for it—or at the very least, curious about it.

Safety first

Before we begin to explore the art of pleasure as a tool for self-discovery and liberation, let's start to set the groundwork for our sense of safety. Safety is required in order for us to open to pleasure; in order for us to look into the ocean of ourselves and see what lies beneath the surface.

There's a chance that within your experience of life so far there have been times you didn't feel safe in your body, or perhaps feeling pleasure wasn't safe for you in some way or another.

Stress can contribute to feeling unsafe within our body. When we are stressed, even if we logically know that we're in a safe environment, our sympathetic nervous system (and the fight-flight-freeze response) is activated and our body believes it should be wary of danger and definitely not surrender to pleasure.

Avoiding pleasure until we've been productive is an indication that on some level we aren't feeling entirely safe to experience pleasure 'prematurely'—i.e. until we've 'earned it' and have ticked off all the to-dos.

So step one is to bring yourself to a place of safety within your body. I invite you to do this before any pleasure practice that feels a little uncomfortable at first.

Take your time, relax your body, and if you still don't have a sense of safety after this, return to it at a later time.

We calm our nervous system, we bring ourselves to the present moment, we notice where we are and that we are safe …

1. Sit somewhere comfortable.
2. Take at least five deep breaths.
3. Bring your sensory practice in—notice the support you feel from where you're sitting, look around and become aware of what's in your environment; take in the smells, sounds, sights.

4. Bring your hands to your body. Touch yourself in a way that feels safe. Maybe give yourself a gentle squeeze, stroke your skin, massage your face. Notice your current connection to the body.
5. Feel into your body and move in any way that feels good and available to you right now. Maybe it's rolling the shoulders, stretching the neck, twisting the spine or bending forward to stretch your back.
6. Remind yourself that you are safe.
7. Now let's play.

Note: You can skip this process once you begin to feel safe in your body with this practice (or if you feel completely comfortable to begin with).

Activity 1
The pleasure genie

Now we've established safety, we can surrender to the practice of using pleasure as the tool for exposing those hidden, unconscious programs. Let me demonstrate what I mean with this exercise.

Please grab your pen and journal and be ready to write down what comes to mind in response to this next question. Jot down everything you can think of, without judgement or questioning, without overthinking.

A MOTHER'S PLEASURE

Chances are you'll have answers ranging from one end of the spectrum to the other, and they are all welcome here. In fact, the more answers you have, the better, even if they seem to contradict each other. That's ok too.

Ok so here we go … write what comes up for you when I ask you this question:

If I were a pleasure genie, how would you feel if I offered you pleasure in every moment of every day—for the rest of your life? What thoughts come up for you?

Chances are you'll have some responses from one end of the spectrum—*Oh awesome, sounds fun! I'd love that! Great!*—some responses from the other end of the spectrum—*How frivolous. I wouldn't deserve it. I'd be ashamed to tell anyone*—and anything and everything in between.

Jot them all down, one after another. Don't read them until you feel like you're done and there's none left to come through right now.

I invite you to repeat this question to yourself throughout the day, maybe over a day or two, and continue to jot down the thoughts and feelings that come up for you. All of it—from what your mother-in-law might say about it, to how embarrassed you might be if you showed your pleasure-filled face publicly, to the question of how you will get anything done.

This is just the start of this practice. This is just the tip of the iceberg that reveals to us our relationship with pleasure and our subconscious programming.

And the best part about it?

You don't have to go searching for all of the experiences, behaviours, attitudes, beliefs, emotional reactions, habits, skills, associative memories, conditioned responses and perceptions that no longer serve you—no mama's got time for that.

What we can do is begin to be driven by desire and led by pleasure. We can begin to say YES to the things that we desire, to the things that will bring us pleasure. This will automatically bring to the surface the things that are holding us back from self-discovery, liberation and our pleasure.

Soul over shoulds

I remember one of the times I started putting this practice into action. After having two babies in two years, I was finally at a stage where I felt I could leave our youngest for a few hours to go out for lunch with some friends. Two hours to sit with my full attention on sharing stories with my friends, with no snacks to provide, no baby to hold, no breastfeeding to be done. That was a pleasure I'd been craving for what felt like months.

As I was heading out the door saying goodbye to Jake and the boys, I was stuck in what I can only describe as mum-guilt friction—where I logically knew it was fine to go out with my friends, that it would benefit me (and the rest of the family), but my mind and body's responses told me otherwise. My mind started bringing up thoughts like, *They're too young to be left with anyone else, You should be looking after them, A good mother is with her children twenty-four seven, Being with your children is more important than lunch with friends.*

Before devoting myself to this practice, I would have ignored my body, tried not to notice the resistive thoughts, numbed the discomfort in my body with a glass of wine, distracted myself with some scrolling or cleaning, or literally pushed the feelings down with food. I would have exhausted myself trying to not feel guilty, and not really enjoyed any time or pleasure that was available to me. The programming would have been left there, unresolved in my subconscious, ready to bring itself to the surface the next time around.

What I discovered is that in deepening my connection to my mind and body, I could hear my soul guiding me towards what she desired—and choose her desires over the 'shoulds'.

So here's what we're going to do.

When you notice a desire arrive, acknowledge it and honour it (take a mental or actual note of it). Get really conscious about what's coming up in your mind and body. If possible, say YES and have, create or experience the thing. HERE is where your cards are shown to you. Here is where the discomfort will likely start to arise. Here is where your mind will begin to turn you away from your desires, and your body will start to feel like an uncomfortable place to be.

When we don't honour these thoughts or feelings, we continue to run the 'default settings', enabling this pattern to resurrect itself every time we have a desire that feels problematic.

In the next chapter we'll explore deeper issues that come from not acknowledging the bodily experience of discomfort and how it prevents us from feeling pleasure, joy and happiness to the depths that we have potential for. There'll likely be more there than just having to carry a sense of mum guilt out to lunch with you.

Activity 2
Add to your Feel-Good Guide

What's something that you feel really called to do or experience at the moment?

Is there something that would bring you pleasure that you have a desire for?

Take a few moments to consider what you'd like to have, create or experience right now and jot it down in your Feel-Good Guide.

Note: Are some things already popping their

heads up? Thoughts that say *I don't have time for that right now, That's not for me, Maybe I'll get to that someday*? Please be curious and non-judgemental, dear reader.

The practice

So, what to do? We allow the things in our subconscious undercurrent to come to the surface every time we have the opportunity to open to pleasure. To do what we desire. To enjoy ourselves. To have fun. To pamper ourselves. Or whatever it is in the moment that our body is drawing us to.

We get conscious about what it is that we desire, and we say yes to the pleasurable thing.

We say yes and we observe what thoughts arise.

We say yes and we feel the feelings that present themselves.

We say yes and we get curious about what comes up that wants to hold us back from our pleasure.

We say yes and we allow ourselves permission to see what thoughts and beliefs we carry, without judgement. Without deciding what is right or wrong. Without looking for someone to blame. Without needing to convince or argue.

For example, you're invited to something or somewhere that would be pleasurable for you. Notice you've been offered the opportunity to open to pleasure. Notice what's coming up in your mind and body. Note down any thoughts or feelings, just like we did earlier—without judgement. Perhaps some are surprising, some are expected.

Summon a sense of safety if it feels really uncomfortable; if you feel like you want to fight, flee or freeze.

From here we get to become really aware of all of those parts that have come up, acknowledge them, love them, integrate them into our body and our psyche, and if we wish, choose something that is more helpful for us.

Remember we are operating from pre-programmed ways of being.

The following is a process that's been helpful for me and my clients in changing the programming and installing the new program. Explore one thought or 'idea' at a time, covering as many as you feel called to.

Note that when you start doing this exercise, there might be a lot more to explore than expected—don't worry, there will end up being less and less.

When faced with the opportunity for pleasure:

1. What thoughts or ideas arise?
2. Are they true?
3. Where did they come from?
4. Do they feel good?
5. Would I like to keep these thoughts or feelings? (If yes, great. Move on with your pleasure activity. If not, keep going.)
6. What would be a better thought or feeling?
7. Every time you catch yourself thinking the old thought, choose to replace it with the new, better

feeling thought. (This is how we replace the old default program with the new one. It can relieve you of mum guilt if you experience it for being self-focussed or doing things that make you feel good.)

What you're being gifted here is insight into your subconscious. You're being shown how you've been socialised and what you've learned along the way about what is allowed to get in the way of your pleasure. You're using your desires and the things that would bring you pleasure as a metaphorical magnifying glass to reveal what's in the way of your pleasure. You're getting to see, maybe for the first time ever, what your relationship to pleasure is, and learn a little more about what informs that for you, as we will all have our own unique relationship to pleasure and meeting our desires.

We don't have to see these parts of us or our interesting ideas, beliefs or truths as problems, blocks or things we need to get rid of. Remember the full-spectrum woman that you are? You are a whole being, perfect as you are in this moment, exactly where you are.

Should you wish to experience more pleasure, then this practice will help you see what's stopping you—not what's good or bad, right or wrong, but just what's there, ready to be acknowledged and accepted with a new kind of programming that will further your self-discovery, pleasure liberation and transformation.

An opportunity to explore

When it comes to being desire driven and prioritising pleasure, what motherhood has taught me over the last few years is this: we are the ones who get to decide what is true for us. We can change our minds and choose something that is more aligned or helpful for us. We can begin to realise that the rules and ideas that we had assumed were true, right and to be adhered to, were actually just the result of previous conditioning—conditioning that we can explore with curiosity and shift if we choose to.

Motherhood is a spiritual journey because of this alone. We have the opportunity to explore our identity, what we believe to be true about the world and the way we move through the world. We get to be conscious of our life and what our values are. Motherhood brings us to a deeper awareness of where we want to spend our time, energy, money, intimacy, passion, attention and other personal resources.

As you consistently and regularly move through the practice we've learned, and continue to become aware of this unconscious undercurrent of thought and programming, you will come to see where your self-worth and internalised societal value lie.

Through this process you will learn to make friends with your desires, say yes to receiving, and enjoy the things that bring you pleasure, without the burden of overwhelming discomfort, guilt and shame. (There'll be more on shame in the next chapter.)

Say yes to receiving,
and enjoy the things that
bring you pleasure.

Chapter ten
PLEASURE PATHWAYS

As mothers, we do such a great job of 'holding it all together' that we've lost the ability to let it all go, to allow feelings to flow.

And flow they must, should we desire any depth of pleasure, love, happiness or whatever it is that would create a life that is enjoyable for us.

The more we hold in our feelings and what's alive for us in our body, the more we prevent ourselves from feeling the full spectrum of emotions that are trying to flow through us.

When we ignore, suppress, numb and distract ourselves from what we really feel, these pathways that could allow pleasure to flow become clogged with contents we're trying to avoid, making what we're trying to avoid more present than ever.

We can find ourselves numb, confused, overwhelmed and desensitised. We might lack the ability to experience presence and pleasure, intimacy in partnership and with life might not permeate past the surface, and we might feel so exhausted from hiding and holding it all together that we miss the opportunity to emotionally purge our way to pleasure.

The fear of sharing your truth

I remember having a maternity-leave coffee date with another mama friend after my first baby was born. (I called it eternity leave and lo and behold six years later I still haven't gone back.) My friend and I were sitting in the sunshine outside at the local cafe, the sound of coffee beans grinding and the juicer juicing, the smell of coffee and chai spice dancing in the air as our two babies, born a few weeks apart, slept beside us.

My friend was asking about my first group support session after my postpartum depression diagnosis.

'What was it like? What did everyone share?'

Well ... I couldn't share other women's stories, but I was also too scared to share mine. (I trusted my friend but still felt ashamed of myself.) So I told her the details of what I had shared, but passed it off as the experiences of others.

'Oh, you know,' I said, 'we just shared the way things were feeling for us. Some people were just really tired and feeling unsupported, some people were angry, and frustrated, feeling grief for their old life and trapped in a new one.'

My friend said, 'That's really sad. To feel trapped, and grief and all of that. That would be so horrible.'

'I know,' I replied.

And I did know. What I knew was that it wasn't meant to be like this.

What I knew was that it was meant to be enjoyable. Lovely. Bliss even.

And yet there I was—tired, feeling unsupported, angry, frustrated, grieving, trapped. And then feeling even more trapped because she didn't understand, and because she felt sorry for the other women (i.e. me). It's only now that I sit here typing this five years later I consider that perhaps she felt the same way, and was too scared to share her feelings with me, just as I was too scared to share mine with her.

Honour the shadows too

As mothers, we know how we're supposed to feel. And if our feelings fall outside of that, we shut them down. We lace them up with shame and tie them tight to our chest. We distract ourselves with coffee dates and feeding apps and cot sheet sets. We numb ourselves with doomscrolling or a daily drip of wine, whatever works, and avoid any conversation where these feelings might expose themselves—for there aren't many safe spaces a mother can typically go to share this side of motherhood. Yet.

And yet there is another side we get to experience as well. Even in my darkest of days, my baby would melt me. I'd be fuming at the sleep deprivation, but a reflexive smile would awaken me as my son's eyes met mine. A gush of love would fill my chest as his dimply hand slid down my arm as he met sleep. I'd feel an unexpected sense of gratitude seeing his tiny clothes hanging from the line.

Mamahood bliss was there, even if it was fleeting. I had had glimpses and I was determined, and hopeful, to find more.

What I discovered was that in the spaces where I felt safe to have those conversations that no one else seemed to be having (in my group support session that I hid behind amongst my friends, it seemed), I was able to do more than just access my grief and sense of being trapped and unsupported; I was able to access deeper layers of joy and contentment—and even pleasure—that didn't feel so fleeting.

As I was purging the shadows from my postpartum Pandora's box, I was purging my way to a pleasure-filled path that I had only just taken my first steps on. I came to realise that we cannot access our desires, our body's intuition, our body's messages or our pleasure if we cannot also be with our discomfort, our disappointment, our sadness and our grief—all of it.

The more I could tap into, honour and experience those feelings that I had been avoiding, suppressing, and distracting myself from, the more I could tap into and experience the feelings that I craved.

Knowing what I know now, it makes total sense.

Our emotional stream

Dr Brené Brown says, 'We cannot selectively numb emotions.

When we numb the painful emotions, we also numb the positive emotions.'

Visualise your pleasurable emotions (joy, contentment, satisfaction, happiness) following all your other less pleasurable emotions down a stream (anger, sadness, grief, frustration). If we aren't letting all of our feelings flow down the stream, they become clumped-up debris that block the flow of ALL our emotions.

If we aren't moving our negative emotions through our body, they will limit the flow of our emotional stream, making it harder for all of those good feelings to stream through as well.

My friend and mentor Carlie Maree said once, 'Flowing water runs clear.' If you want to feel the pristine emotions of pleasure, you'll also need to move those that are less pleasurable and socially welcome.

If you've ever breastfed (or used a breast pump) you'll know exactly what I mean. If we don't let it flow regularly—if we don't express or feed when the milk is produced in response to a suckling baby or breast pump, a baby crying, or feeling love for our little ones, for example—then our milk will build up and impact flow, and we risk creating blocked ducts and potentially a lot of discomfort and pain.

When we express what's alive and present in our emotional stream, it will allow a deeper, clearer stream to flow. It will allow us to more easily access clearer, deeper, more pleasurable emotions—the ones that feel good, that make parenting and motherhood more enjoyable. The ones that allow us to connect more intimately with those we love most, and simply experience joy in our world.

So just like our breastfeeding/pumping situation—express regularly, let it flow, respond to what is happening inside your body.

Find a sense of safety in order to enhance expression—whether that be in a group support setting, with a friend or partner you feel safe around, with a professional who is skilled in providing this support, or in a private safe space alone—and welcome the magic that follows; the electric current that will begin to hum gently through your body, reminding you that you are alive and connected to the ecstatic current of life.

Healthy expression

Emotions are energy in motion, so in order for us to express them, we must move them through and out of us. Some ways will be healthier and more helpful than others (screaming at your children probably isn't how you want to express yourself), so here are some examples of what you can do to move emotions through you in order to feel the full spectrum of life:

- Movement: Shake your body, stomp your feet, take a baseball bat to the bed, dance, move freely as your body pleases.
- Sound: Scream, roar, moan or sigh into a pillow, letting any other kind of sound come out.
- Process: Have conversations, journal, write, attend a women's circle.

Pleasure and shame

One of the strongest emotions limiting us from experiencing pleasure is (often unconsciously) shame.

As humans, we are naturally motivated by pleasure (through spikes in dopamine within our body) as it enhances our progress and evolution as a species. The friction comes when we are met with a pleasure- and sex-shaming society.

As most of us have been overtly and subtly shamed for seeking and experiencing pleasure since we were small children, we have experienced pleasure and shame bonded together. When our natural drive towards pleasure brings us closer to it, it brushes us up against programmed feelings of shame. (This can then often lead to compulsive behaviours that act as a coping mechanism to protect us from the shame, but keep us distanced from our desires and our pleasure. More on that later.)

Think of the phrases *Does she have no shame!* and *She's totally shameless!* In our society, shame is seen as something women are required to have, to keep us 'in check'—to make us humble, good girls. The thing is, shame is holding us back from the platter of pleasure that our life has to offer.

When I work with clients who want to release shame, I use a neurolinguistic programming (NLP) technique that taps them into their subconscious mind, and takes them back to the first event where they experienced shame. *Every single time* I've gone there with a client, the first event in which they felt shame was in relation to experiencing pleasure (usually when they were very young).

They were shamed for eating something they weren't supposed to eat, or that someone else thought was disgusting. Shamed for taking something when it wasn't theirs to take. Shamed for touching their body. And shamed for any other number of things because someone else decided it was wrong, disgusting, naughty, bad.

What follows is usually repetitive shaming for experiencing pleasure in childhood that then becomes a learned process into adulthood.

Repetitive shaming linked with pleasure strengthens the shame–pleasure bond. So in adult life, both external influences as well as ourselves are actively policing and shaming us for desiring or experiencing pleasure.

The shame–pleasure bond becomes so deeply ingrained in the subconscious that we become unaware of the shame that arises when we near pleasure; perhaps only registering an uncomfortable shift within our body that we want to escape from or get rid of, so we might use coping mechanisms such as compulsive behaviours to numb and create distance from the emotion.

Common compulsive behaviours include:

- Constant content consumption—e.g. Instagram/Facebook/podcasts
- Excessive cleaning
- Overeating
- Overspending
- Obsessing over diet, exercise or weight
- Drinking too much

Creating new pathways

The good news is that we can break the cycle. We can rid ourselves of unnecessary shame–pleasure bonding and open up another pathway for pleasure to reach us.

Even if you don't do an NLP shame-release experience to uncouple the very first shame–pleasure bond, even if you're not sure when your first experience was, even if you're not sure which events contributed to strengthening the shame–pleasure bond over your lifetime, you can still begin to uncouple those bonds, neutralise the charge around the shame, release it and the associated discomfort, and welcome pleasure into all aspects of your life.

This is helpful both when there are compulsive behaviours present in your life and when there are not.

When we neutralise the charge around the shame, we have an opportunity to open to and experience pleasure, clear the compulsion, and actually feel satiated by smaller amounts of what we have previously been consuming to excess. For example, instead of eating a whole packet of chocolate biscuits, we can eat one or two, be with the pleasure of that, and not reach for more and more. Consuming the whole packet of biscuits can be a way to numb the shame that comes up when we begin to tap into pleasure. You begin to do less.

Perhaps you'll begin to notice that the obsessive content consumption becomes a shorter session of social self-care or inspiration; the excessive cleaning becomes acceptance or contentment amongst the chaos some days; the overeating becomes an experience driven by desire and taste that is satiating after a much smaller amount than usual; or the compulsive alcohol consumption becomes a joyful glass of wine instead of the whole bottle.

What's helped me to do this in my own experience and with my clients?

- Making the unconscious conscious.
- Feeling the discomfort of shame arise in the moments where pleasure presents itself.
- Exploring and practising different ways to express the felt sense of shame (and discomfort) when it arises.
- Journalling it out to receive clarity around it.
- Speaking to your shame.
- Asking where your shame has come from, and what information it has for you.
- Asking the childhood version of you within what she needs to hear and feel instead of the shame she received.
- Reminding yourself that you are made for meeting your desires, that it is safe to experience pleasure, that you are allowed to hold pleasure in your body.
- Replacing shame with what you need to hear and feel instead. Maybe this looks like speaking to your childhood self in the mirror. Maybe it is literally giving yourself a hug. Maybe it is following through with the pleasure you desire and repetitively reminding yourself that you are safe; pleasure is for you.

Breaking the cycle

Imagine if every child on Earth witnessed their parents prioritising their pleasure; meeting their needs; filling their cup with what they desire; being less reactive and more responsive; having deeper intimacy with their partner and loved ones; and having enough trust in themselves and their intuition (through being deeply connected with their body) that they parent and do life in a way they are solid on. Imagine what could change for them and how our society would look as they grow into adults and potentially parents themselves.

Imagine the change of societal expectations and the resolving of shame that could be waiting for our children as they make their way into adulthood and parenthood. What our sons or daughters could provide for the future mother of their children and what our daughters would expect of their co-parent partners.

This is the world that you are contributing to simply by devoting yourself to a more pleasurable path. Simply from reading this book and putting these practices to use in your life. Simply by meeting this part of your life now, and not 'when you have time' or 'when the kids are at school' or 'when the kids are grown,' etc.

Because you are doing this work, it means you have healed parts of your lineage behind you and in front of you.

Because you are doing this work, it means your children won't have to; you are modelling this to your children so they'll know how to express themselves in a way that is helpful and how to prioritise their pleasure.

Because you are doing this work, it means our society will begin to shift to one that does not shame others for experiencing and prioritising pleasure, but welcomes the full-spectrum self and celebrates the person who is connected to their pleasure and actively creating a life they enjoy.

You are alive and
connected
to the ecstatic
current of life.

Chapter eleven
THROUGH THE BODY

Before my marriage and three kids, a guy I had just slept with made a comment about my body. We were still in that post-climactic, euphoric pleasure bubble, on a hot night, mid-summer. I had come out of a long-term relationship feeling liberated in more ways than one.

I was feeling glorious as we lay there together, entwined and sweaty, when he looked me all over and said, 'You're very well proportioned!'

Not *You're beautiful/amazing/hot AF* ... no. Well proportioned.

I cringed. Did you just cringe then too?

Like someone had popped the pleasure bubble with a pin, I contracted, wanted to cover my well-proportioned body and run away somewhere safe. WTF, I thought. *Nice one, dickhead. Last time I sleep with him!*

We could probably all start to slam the guy, saying what a prick he was. (Or how unobservant he was—I actually have a pretty short torso and really long limbs.) And chances are we've all had that conversation with our friends, hating on the arsehole who didn't make nice comments about our bodies. But you know what? We probably say or have said worse to ourselves.

It's likely that a lot of the critiquing and criticism our bodies have received has come from within us. Potentially from unachievable patriarchal standards for beauty, but ultimately from ourselves.

The harm that we've caused our bodies through criticism, or other means, takes us further and further from the deep connection that is available to us.

If we were to have a partner that abused us, chances are we would not have a deeply connected, intimate relationship with them. There'd be no good communication or support for each other. It's the same with our body.

If we can honour her, connect with her, value, witness and listen to her, we will have a closely connected, intimate relationship with her, with great communication and support for each other.

Our body is the portal to pleasure.

If we are disconnected from our body, we are disconnected from our pleasure. If we feel unsafe in our body, we'll feel unsafe receiving pleasure. If we contract, close up and put layers between ourselves and our body, we increase the distance between us and our pleasure.

If we truly want to experience greater pleasure, we need to have greater reverence for our body. We need to foster a deeper relationship with her. We need not tell her she's well-proportioned, but bow at her feet and worship her for the goddess that she is. For the life she has created, the baby she has birthed. The life she has nurtured.

Now is our chance.

In this chapter we're going to explore different ways to deepen our reverence for and relationship to our body, so that we can bring more pleasure into our world.

If you're anything like me or the women I grew up with, you've had your fair share of body shaming—likely from others, especially from yourself. And if you're a mother, there really is a lot stacked against you, from the high societal expectations we feel we should meet; to the systemic abuse most have been exposed to; to the self-sacrificial story we're told to play out; to the messaging around our bodies we receive from such a young age that then often contributes to the deterioration of this relationship with our body. While we may feel soft as we enter postpartum, it can feel like there's no soft place left to land.

Birthing bodies

I remember when my sister had her first baby, my niece. I was twenty-five and had no idea that your belly doesn't just go back to how it was pre-baby the moment the baby comes out. That for the first few days and weeks a mama's uterus is still making its way back to pre-baby size. How had I lived for twenty-five years, as a female who would potentially birth children myself, and not known that your belly would remain looking beautifully pregnant as it shrinks back to its pre-pregnancy size?

A relative came in for her visit and, like me, obviously had no idea that was something that happened as she had exclaimed, 'OMG you still look pregnant!'

Everyone's reaction to her comment told me that it was not a good thing to point out or remind a mother of her postpartum body, because we are expected to *bounce back* to our pre-baby body and if that hasn't happened, we certainly shouldn't bring awareness to it.

I was very aware of this expectation, particularly after giving birth for the first time. It wasn't that I was shamed or spoken to negatively about my body—it was the opposite, which conveyed the same message: your body is here to be objectified and should be aesthetically pleasing for others' pleasure, not your own.

I was a few months into motherhood when I was clinically depressed, suffering anxiety and insomnia, and had so many people congratulate me on how I was doing so well, looking the way I looked when I'd just had a baby!

'Well done you!'

I was even called a bitch for 'putting others to shame'. It's such a weird thing to navigate. I remember feeling like it was an insult—or at least an empty compliment—and such an insufficient summation of the magic of a birthing body.

So although I was already mentally, physically and emotionally unwell, feeling totally depleted and defeated, I was also aware that my body was something additional that carried expectation, invited judgement and continued on the journey of objectification.

A story of reverence

What if postpartum became less about how much we scrutinise, contort and try to mould our bodies (perhaps into what they used to be), and more about how much kindness, love and pleasure we could give and receive from our bodies. What if our bodies were revered for what they were doing and had done in giving birth, instead of how they looked and what clothes they could fit back into?

What if we went there now?

What if we began to rewrite a story of reverence for our birthing bodies that surpasses the superficial and seeps into the sacred?

That's the conversation I want to have.

What if, instead of focussing on the way we looked, we focussed on the way we loved ourselves, and welcomed others to love us too?

What if, instead of grabbing at folds of belly with thoughts of dissatisfaction and disgust, we held our belly safe in our hands and proclaimed our love and appreciation for it?

What if, instead of looking in the mirror with critical shaming words, we gave our body a mental shout-out instead? (*Hey, gorgeous!*)

What if, instead of mourning our pre-baby breasts and deciding where they've changed for the worse, we massaged them with warming oils and kind words?

Might all that actually begin to bring some pleasure in itself? Might it even start to mend some of the hurt that's been inflicted on her over the years from both society and ourselves? Might it help us to build a bridge back home to our bodies, where we are in such deep communion with her that we're able to listen to her and revere her?

A mother's intuition

Part of the reason we might have trouble feeling anything that we want to feel—including pleasure, joy, desire and satisfaction—is the objectification of and disconnection from our bodies at best, and distaste and distrust for our bodies at worst.

What we've been diverted from as we compare and scrutinise our bodies is the knowledge that the body is our portal to pleasure. That when we are connected to our body, we are connected to Source/consciousness/God itself. That it is the body that informs us of our boundaries; our intuition; and all of the messages that help us feel as though we are dancing through our days, and beautifully navigating our nights. Whether this be the physical information we receive from her (thumping heart and shortness of breath when we're stressed or anxious, our sympathetic nervous system activating in response to danger, our electrified full-body hum and tingling yoni when we are turned on) or the mental information we receive as a thought or 'mother's intuition' (from the voice that says *Don't take the kids to the party; they're tired and it will be a disaster,* to the sense that there is something wrong with our children even when no one else believes us).

I remember the day my mother's intuition was so loud

that even doctors and other hospital staff couldn't sway me.

It was a week after my son's first birthday. He fell off a swing onto a rubber mat at the playground. I knew something was wrong, and even as he was wheeled through the hospital smiling with dried-up tears, loving the excitement, I honoured my intuition and pressed for an x-ray. The doctors explained how unlikely it was that he had broken anything, that they were ninety-nine per cent sure there wasn't a fracture.

Safe to say the doctors who thought I was being an overzealous helicopter parent sheepishly apologised before declaring he had a broken leg.

What does this have to do with pleasure? In my experience, the better the connection we have with our bodies, the better connection we have to our intuition and the messages our body is conveying to us. The better connection we have with our intuition and the messages our body is giving us, the greater sense of ease and pleasure we can draw from our days.

When we have fostered a strong relationship with our body:

- we are more aware of what's pleasurable for us
- we are conscious of our desires as they drop in
- we can be informed by the physical responses of our body
- we have a greater ability to heighten the sensation we feel
- we have the capacity to traverse greater depths of pleasure

- we can be physically present in each and every moment (which is where pleasure resides—in the NOW)

You cannot experience pleasure outside a place of presence.

Feeling the body

When I was recovering from perinatal mood disorders, I took myself to a naked yoga class—not one's typical activity to recover from something like that, but an appropriate response for me nonetheless.

After walking into the candlelit room—think soft lighting, soothing sounds and scattered rose petals—we chose a place to lie down, and were instructed to close our eyes and slowly de-robe when we were ready, allowing our bodies to be felt by ourselves. I'd say it was probably around twenty minutes or so of just lying there; I let the soft music wash over me and felt every inch of my body—not as a performance, not to achieve anything or reach any goal, but simply to feel my body, and allow my body to feel. I was giving to myself, for myself, for no other purpose than seeing what that felt like, and experiencing pleasure.

I came away from that night wondering why I had never offered myself the time to touch all of myself, when it's available to me in every second of every day. Why hadn't I given myself the opportunity to enjoy my body, to learn what I like, to receive without any expectation of giving? I had thought I was body confident, body aware, and very connected to my body, so outside of the quick 'self-pleasure for the purpose of achieving climax'. Why had I never thought to receive pleasure at the altar of my body with my own hands?

We have these incredible bodies with the ability to feel the full spectrum of sensations. The ability to give and receive pleasure is literally at our fingertips, on the tip of our tongue, in all of our senses. Why is this not something that is taught, modelled, spoken about, encouraged and celebrated?

From that night I became devoted to feeling my body more. Not to perform for anyone, not to reach the goal of orgasm, not to seduce anyone—not for anyone else's pleasure, but for my own. For my own healing, my own comfort, my own relationship building with my body.

Sometimes it's like having a meandering cup of tea with a dear old friend; other times it's familiarising myself with newer landscapes of my body, feeling parts that seem to have shifted by the seasons of life. Sometimes it's the access point to layers of body shaming I thought I'd released, and I realise that I have another layer to expose and peel away.

Activity 1
Exploration through self-touch

So, dear reader, I invite you to begin. Begin with this ritual of building a bridge back home to your body; begin to feel your body and allow it to feel.

Start with setting yourself a widow of five to ten minutes for self-touch without being goal oriented, and see what happens. See what comes up. See what is alive for you each time. See it as an exploration of parts of yourself that you had previously ignored, suppressed or numbed, parts that are there to share themselves with you. Meet them, welcome them, and allow them to show you what lies there.

You might like to move these parts, thoughts or feelings through you, as we did in our last chapter, by means of expression: through sounds, movement, crying, singing or journalling, for example.

Preparing for pleasure

Just like any relationship where there has been disconnection, there is always opportunity for repair and healing.

Read on for three of the simplest, most easily accessible and most potent practices I've used and share in my programs and mentoring to bow at the altar of our body. To build deeper intimacy, foster a stronger relationship and enhance sensitisation with her.

To begin any or all of these, intention and process is everything. As mentioned earlier in the book, the masculine is goal oriented, while the feminine is process oriented, so we want to move with our feminine energy for these practices.

Instead of simply following the steps through to completion as a 'boxed ticked, move on to the next one' kind of practice, I invite you to make each activity an intentional ritual, devoted to honouring your body and your portal to pleasure. They can be brief rituals, and can also take a lot of time if you have it available to you. The focus is on what is alive for you throughout the process; on generating the connection, energy and presence available to you, without any need for performative or goal-oriented elements.

You might find all or a combination of the following actions pleasurable and useful when opening to these rituals. They might make up a big part of the process.

As you prepare to begin:

- Bring your awareness to the present moment and notice what you notice. Turn on your senses, feeling grounded in the physical, 3D space you're in.
- Ensure you feel safe in your environment and in your body. Do what you need to do to feel safe and comfortable to initiate and move through these rituals. As discussed in Chapter Nine, this might include reminding yourself you're safe; bringing safe, conscious touch to your body; and focussing on steady breathing. Continue to check back in with yourself as you go.

- Close your eyes. Turn your focus inward. Towards what's going on in your mind, your body. Consider how you're feeling—physically, emotionally, mentally, energetically. Notice anything that comes up. Observe without judgement.
- Invite some intuitive movement in to awaken your body and initiate your connection. It could be gently rolling your head to loosen a tight neck; it could be arching your spine while on hands and knees, making circles with your hips, stretching anywhere that feels tight, breathing into any areas of tension or desired focus.

Activity 2
Breast massage

For better breast love and opening of your heart and radiant centre, open to breast massage. Either in the shower, or somewhere else that feels private and safe, spend a few minutes giving yourself a breast massage.

Step 1

Make it intentional. Focus on generating love and bringing it to your breasts.

Step 2

Tune into the present moment. Focus on the now.

Step 3

Using a nourishing body wash or warming oils, intuitively cup, stroke and massage your breasts as you please. Notice what does and doesn't feel good and bring some kind words to the surface for your breasts and body.

Step 4

Create affirmations that you can repeat regularly that feel good, and not "far fetched"

This can also be done for other parts of your body you'd like to bring love to.

Activity 3
Surrender to the sun

For yoni activation and all-over goddess vibes, Surrender to the Sun.

This can be a very activating experience, edging us towards the limits of our comfort zone.

Step 1

Find a spot outside to receive the full spectrum of light from the sun. Place some rugs, cushions or pillows down for comfort.

Step 2

Take a few deep breaths. Imagine breathing life into your yoni. Turn your focus inward and invite some movement.

Step 3

When you feel ready, slowly remove your pants and underwear.

Step 4

Lie with full exposure on your yoni.

Step 5

Consciously invite an energy of relaxation. Take conscious breaths, directing focus to your yoni. (And be sure not to burn yourself; start with less than two minutes to begin with.)

Activity 4
Seduce yourself

This is going to help you feel empowered to realise that you have the greatest effect when it comes to feeling loved and turned on—whether that be erotically, or for life in general. If you practise this more than once (and I invite you to), it's likely you'll go on a deeper journey into loving yourself each time and discovering more pleasure on the other side of this activity, even if not-so-pleasurable feelings arise.

Step 1

Create a private space and time for yourself in front of a mirror, maybe with candles or dim lighting, rugs and cushions. Play some music that feels seductive to your ears and feels good to move to.

Step 2

Receive yourself in front of the mirror as you take your time moving as you please. Slowly undress and notice anything and everything that you love about your body.

Step 3

Remind yourself that you are safe. Look into your eyes and say to yourself, 'I love you,' even if it feels hard. Even if you don't feel like you believe it yet.

Step 4

Bring safe, loving touch to your body if you wish. There's no rush. Slow down.

Step 5

Notice any unhelpful or hurtful comments about your body that arise and offer yourself love each time. Remind yourself of what you love about your body.

Step 6

It's just you alone with your beautiful body. Be kind. Go gently. Take your time. Do what feels safe and loving for you.

Step 7

Once you feel complete or your available time is up, literally hug yourself and say 'I love you' one last time before re-dressing, or not re-dressing.

Step 8

Remember all of the things that you love about yourself, and write them down to remind yourself through your days.

Our body is the portal to pleasure.

Chapter twelve
PARENTING WITH PLEASURE

Because I wanted to be the most selfless, devoted, 'good' mother that ever existed—which was well-intentioned but led to an unhealthy place for me and my family—I would prioritise my children's pleasure at every turn. If we drove somewhere in the car, I'd play The Wiggles. If I was planning the day, we'd do what the kids wanted to do. If I had some time and space while they napped, I'd fold the washing so I could be present for their desires when they were awake. If I was cooking dinner, I'd make what the children loved to eat.

I made their preferences my priority—and whilst that's a no-brainer for a lot of things as a parent, when we make someone else's preferences our priority all the time, we miss out on the pleasures of our own.

I began to make small changes at first: playing my

favourite playlist on the way to day care, folding washing in the sun as the kids played outside, napping or doing something I enjoyed at rest time, donning headphones and strapping them into the double stroller to enjoy a podcast or audiobook. When I opened to reclaiming simple pleasures for myself, I was then able to gift myself pleasures that felt more luxurious and even audacious.

Feel free to borrow my simple pleasures mentioned in this chapter and add them to your Feel-Good Guide. Now we're going to go deeper than enjoying ourselves by participating in self-care around our children; we're going to look at what can impact our experience of pleasure when actively parenting (and mothering in general), and explore HOW we can make parenting and mothering in general more pleasurable.

The motherhood we desire

When we stop separating pleasure and parenting, we get to create a more respectful, intimate and loving connection with our children, and experience the motherhood of our desires.

Consider the times you've not felt proud of your parenting. Chances are you were feeling depleted, unsupported, drained—running on empty.

As we know now, being able to access and receive pleasure is a major contributor to filling our cup and fuelling our tank—allowing us to feel more nourished and resourced, and less likely to react in ways we don't feel good about.

As you start to prioritise your pleasure and weave pleasure practices into your life, you'll begin to notice a few things that change in association with parenting.

Change #1

You'll feel more resourced. You'll feel like you have a much fuller cup. You will have a greater capacity to hold emotion and greater emotional intelligence. You will be more creative and think of novel ways to do things. You'll have a greater capacity to be with your emotions and therefore have a greater capacity to be with those of your children too, cultivating a greater sense of ease in parenting.

When we are more resourced, we also have a much higher *reactive threshold*. What this means is that you're more likely to respond to your children instead of react when they do something that 'pushes your buttons'. It means that there is a larger buffer between your children triggering an emotional response in you, and you reacting to that event, which means you're more likely to take a breath, remain calm, not activate the sympathetic (fight or flight) nervous system and respond in a way that feels aligned and respectful. This in itself allows for greater cohesion, stronger trust and deeper levels of connection with your child (as well as any other intimate relationship).

Change #2

You'll indirectly be teaching/modelling the importance of pleasure, self-worth and self-nurturance to your children, and will likely notice your children creating opportunities for, expecting and encouraging your pleasures.

Not long after I started prioritising my pleasure, my two-year-old son started prioritising my pleasure too. He started to point out sunny spots for me to sit in, offer me cups of 'tea' he had made for me, and suggest playing my favourite music in the kitchen on the mornings it slipped my mind. He was seeing the importance of my pleasure and enjoyed the energy it created in our home. He probably preferred the lift in my mood and began supporting me in it.

Change #3

When you have been honouring your needs, welcoming your desires, offering yourself pleasure and owning your pleasure, you'll begin fostering a greater awareness of and stronger relationship with your body.

When you are deeply connected with your body, you are able to easily access your body's wisdom, which includes information about relating to others, knowing your boundaries, making decisions and accessing your intuition (for mamas this one is huge—a mother's intuition is one of her superpowers), along with a whole range of really flippin' impactful strategies for making parenting pleasurable.

Unpacking your triggers

In building greater awareness of your body, you'll become more aware of the times that you're triggered when parenting. The times that feel the opposite of pleasurable. You'll become really aware of where your boundaries lie before they're crossed, instead of simply knowing when they've been crossed (and it's too late to respond differently). You'll be aware of the yellow flags, before they become orange flags, before they become red flags, which again contributes to a greater reactive threshold.

As we know from earlier chapters, most of our day is set by unconscious programs, and until we become conscious of those unconscious programs, we will keep running them. Meaning, what you believe about your children and the way you respond to them are mostly unconscious and unlikely to change unless you become aware of them.

Think about what bothers you most when parenting/mothering your children. What really pushes your buttons? Grinds your gears? Is it when your child seems rude, entitled or impatient? When they act ungrateful? When they make a mess or make loud noises? (Audio-sensitive mums with children who self-soothe with noise will know where I'm coming from!)

I invite you to notice how what triggers one parent might not trigger another, whether that be in your parenting partnership or amongst a group of parents. There's a reason why some things my children do cause me friction, but do not bother their father or another caregiver.

Our children are activating unhealed parts of ourselves that we have previously rejected either consciously or unconsciously.

I was self-conscious about being too loud when I was younger, so when my first toddler got excited and loud (which was often), I found it hard to embrace, whereas his caregivers at day care loved his 'enthusiasm'—this was a prompt for me to heal that part of myself I had disowned. And because it bothered me, it was also something that I found myself focussing my attention on—both what I was seeing as a problem, and what I hadn't healed in myself.

Consider this: What is it that you feel triggered or activated by with your children at the moment?

Why might this bother you?

Is there a history of this story in your life?

Does it open old wounds for you?

Can you embrace the part of you that's been brought to the surface?

Can you see how those parts of you have benefitted you previously? Consider the drawbacks if that part of you hadn't existed.

I began to embrace the loud part of me. I also stopped focussing on the parts of my child that triggered me the most, because when I did focus on them, I would fail to notice when he was doing or being the opposite. I wanted to find the evidence of a well-balanced child, who wasn't just 'not loud' but chill AF—this seemed totally impossible and unlikely, but I focussed on seeing him as chill AF anyway.

And you know what happened? It seemed like he became a lot more chill.

The thing is, he hadn't changed, what had changed was my perception of him and what I was focussing on. I noticed the times he was sitting quietly in his room, flicking through his books (albeit naked). I noticed the times he would come into our bed in the early hours of the morning and snuggle in. I noticed the moments he was listening to another tell a story. I noticed when he was the most settled kid at playgroup (even if only for a few moments).

Whilst I am no parenting expert, what I know to be true from my own experience, and from quantum physics, is that—when it comes to anything—what we focus on, we find evidence for.

Activity 1
Shift your focus

Ever wondered why, when you're focussed on finding money, you'll find it? Or when you've noticed someone is annoying, then everything they do annoys you? It's the same when you focus on your child's 'problem behaviour'. That's the thing you'll notice the most; it'll push your buttons, and it certainly won't make parenting pleasurable.

So how can we shift our focus to something that creates a more pleasurable parenting experience? We consider what it is we want to see and experience in our parenting and we focus on that.

Journal prompts

- What do you want to find the evidence

for in your parenting experience? (e.g. *My kids listen. They rarely fight. I feel calm even when they make the house messy.*)
- What do you want to notice in your children?
- What do you want to witness in the way you parent them?

Activity 2
Reframe your thoughts

Our time as parents of young children is limited, so we may as well do what we can to enjoy them, right?

Here is a list of new, reframed thoughts crafted by myself or my clients that have been helpful in creating a life we want to find the evidence of. Perhaps some will be helpful for you too.

You might have a hard time believing yourself to begin with, so you can either take baby steps, upping the ante each time, or do my favourite thing and times it by ten!

I did this when I was changing the way I felt about the upcoming birth of my third child. The birth of my second was, as I called it, fast and furious. The experience I wanted for my third birth was a pleasant one, and so I timesed my desire by ten and focussed instead on having an orgasmic birth.

By the time it came to birthing my daughter, I had found lots of evidence that her birth could be orgasmic, and integrated the belief that this was available to me. I ended up having the most ecstatic birthing experience. I'll admit that it wasn't orgasmic, but it was a lot better than pleasant!

Reframes you might like to play with include:

- *They're driving me insane* becomes *I love this beautiful chaos*
- *I can't cope with this* becomes *I can breathe through this*
- *Tidy house, tidy mind* becomes *The more mess, the more I feel like myself*
- *I am so alone* becomes *I am always supported*
- *Parenting is hard* becomes *Parenting is effortless* (ok, you might like to upgrade this reframe one step at a time and add in-between *Parenting is getting easier*)
- *My child is doing my head in* becomes *My child is doing their best*
- *Fuck this shit* becomes *This shit doesn't bother me*

The more you can remind yourself of these new thoughts and repeat them, the more they become your default thoughts, and the more they become the reality that you believe and the evidence that you will find. It's not until you believe something is possible that you take action to make it possible.

Don't believe me? Have a go for yourself. Some thoughts might take longer to change if they've been conditioned into your psyche and your body since you were really young; others might not take long at all.

It might not always be easy, but it is simple!

Meaning matters

Whilst we know that the body is the portal to pleasure (that we can deepen our connection with the body to create a heightened sense of pleasure, experience sensuality and more), what we think about something impacts the level of pleasure we experience in association with it too.

Humans are essentialists, meaning it might not just be the taste, feel, smell, sound or sight that brings us pleasure, but also the knowledge of where it has come from, what it's made of, the value of it, or what that experience means for us. It means that our pleasure can be affected by what we believe about the experience.

Does the cup of tea that someone else makes for you taste better than ones you've made yourself? Does two minutes of the sun on your face feel better during 'me time' than it does during the school run? Does a handcrafted, gifted oil blend or candle smell even more delicious than one you could just grab off the shelf from the store?

The essence behind something contributes to the way we feel about it, and therefore can affect the level of pleasure we experience.

Paul Bloom speaks to essentialism and pleasure using the 'in bed' analogy, where it is not just the physical experience that you have when having sex with someone that determines the pleasure you feel—what also affects your pleasure is who you believe you're sleeping with. If they turned out not to be who you thought they were, or their relationship status wasn't what you thought it was, that would affect your pleasure. (For example, if the person you were sleeping with turned out to be your long-lost uncle, THAT will affect your pleasure.)

The same goes for wine. There's an age-old experiment where wine poured from a really expensive-looking bottle will be reported as more enjoyable than wine poured from a cheap bottle—even if they are of the same value, or even the same wine. When it comes to pleasure, it's not just what is experienced that matters; it's what is believed.

This goes to show that pleasure is not solely dependent on the sensations of the body; what we make things *mean* makes a difference to the level of pleasure we experience. So not only does it help to prioritise pleasure in parenting and motherhood; it also helps to consider what we can make it all mean.

Society has a big role to play in this. The socially accepted role of mothering is unglamorous, monotonous, mundane, overwhelming and hard (and yet we're also supposed to love it, lol), and as we know from the start of this book, social narratives are imprinted on us, conditioned and ingrained unconsciously throughout life. So because the meaning of an experience can affect our pleasure, and because we've likely internalised an unpleasant meaning about motherhood, it means that our base level of pleasure when mothering doesn't start at zero, but in the negative. It means it's harder to experience a pleasure-filled motherhood to begin with, because we assume that it isn't.

Activity 3
Embody your values

So what can we do? We can change what we believe about mothering to something that improves the value of it in our minds, which requires effort, given that mothering isn't valued highly, if at all, in our Western society.

Here's what will help improve your experience of pleasure in parenting:

- Consider some of your top values that you associate with pleasure. Maybe they are surrender, sensation, spontaneity, novelty and creativity.
- Identify the ways that parenting, mothering or being a mother allows you to accommodate or accentuate those top values.

A MOTHER'S PLEASURE

One of my top values in relation to pleasure is FREEDOM. Society would have you think that mothering three small children is the opposite of freedom, right? But what helps me to experience more pleasure is deciding that motherhood is pleasurable and has an element of freedom. When I believe that to be true, I subconsciously seek and find where I feel free throughout the day.

In Australia we experienced months of lockdown in 2021, and you'd expect that most mothers—who had been home with their children, not having their usual freedoms—were feeling less free during that time. I knew that if I was going to get through lockdown in a way that didn't deplete me, in a way that I enjoyed, one of the things I would need to experience is freedom. So I began to notice where I could feel freer throughout my day.

I'll never forget the feeling of freedom one afternoon after I pulled up to my mum's house to check in on her. My sons ran down the driveway to the back of the house, while baby girl was perched on my hip. As I walked towards the back door, the breeze picked up and caressed my face, making my hair dance. I noticed my bare feet meeting the ground beneath them. I felt the piercing presence of the moment; I felt such freedom and pleasure. It was as simple and as complex as that.

Activity 4
What wonderful things

Lastly, when we get conscious of and present enough in the here and now, we get to access a portal to infinite possibility. We have the power to choose the lens with which we see the world, see our children, see our family and experience parenting.

The more you can integrate this work, the more evidence you'll find of the reality you desire. The more you'll be motivated to continue to create it, until one day parenting with pleasure becomes more natural than not.

My final invitation to you in this chapter is: be willing, and curious enough, to be open to the idea of unlimited possibility, and start to ponder:

- What wonderful things might be playing out in this reality that I have missed?
- What wonderful opportunities might be around the corner?
- What wonderful support is available to me?
- What wonderful experiences with my children might be possible?
- What wonderful parts of my children am I not noticing?

Be willing, and
curious enough,
to be open to the idea
of unlimited possibility.

Chapter thirteen
ANCHORING PLEASURE

There's a picture of a church from a little village in Greece. It hangs on the wall in the home of one of my clients, Mary. It's where her grandparents were married, but the significance of the picture isn't just about that. It's about what it reminds her of. It's about the way she feels when she looks at that picture. Every time she has holidayed in Greece, she has felt what she once thought was the pulse of Athens, but now refers to as the pulse of her soul.

When she looks at that picture, she's flooded with the feelings of being a young, carefree woman in a foreign country; having new experiences; feeling at ease, fresh and alive. For Mary, this picture is an anchor to those feelings. An anchor that immediately takes her back to her young, carefree, soul-pulsing self—without requiring a trip to Athens.

This is an example of an anchor. If, like me, you heard a baby's cry in the newly postpartum stage and got a let-down, the cry was an anchor to your let-down, even if it wasn't your baby.

You might have had this experience before too. The song that reminds you of that summer you fell in love takes you back to that state of new love, with sun-kissed cheeks and salt in your hair. The turn-on (or repulsion) you feel when you smell the cologne or deodorant of a past lover. The feel of the soft part of your child's neck that takes you back to the early postpartum days and fills you with wonder and softness and love all over again.

What this signifies is that we can anchor in a feeling, and revisit it or light it up, without the actual event that created it in the first place.

Anchors are everywhere

We have anchors everywhere, natural ones that we wouldn't even be aware of, unless we started to look for them. And we are setting up anchors for ourselves and our children all the time.

Like when you have a bedtime routine that includes lavender in the diffuser, a snuggly bear for the babe and a certain lullaby playing. It is something that will remind your child of sleep, prepare them for sleep, and bring about the state of sleepiness. (Looking back now, I wish I'd followed my own suggestions here—we could've used some sleep anchors in the toddler years, especially for our boys!)

A MOTHER'S PLEASURE

When I started to learn about anchors, I began to look for the ones that were already (unconsciously) set up in my life—feeling loved with a morning coffee from the hubs; lighting a candle in devotion for each client I met with; and now, opening my laptop to the same binaural beats track that helps me focus on writing this book.

Just as someone else's baby's cry can induce a let-down for me, and the picture of the church brings on the feelings of actually being in Athens for Mary, our bodies can recreate a reaction within us from external stimuli.

We feel from within

When Mary was telling me about the picture of the church in one of our sessions together, she said, 'I want to feel like I've felt when in Athens, but I obviously can't be in Athens all of the time!' And the good news I gave her was that she didn't need to go there again to feel those feelings; she could simply create an anchor to them. And that's how she realised she had already created an anchor to her Athenian self: the picture of the church.

I love it so much when clients' goals are state oriented. As in, it's a feeling they desire: happiness, contentment, calm, the feeling of being in Athens, etc. Because we can actually have immediate access to that state. It's from within ourselves that we feel these things—we just need to create the right stimulus and know a couple of simple steps, and we have the power to call on that state as desired. This is how we anchor it in.

As you please

Now that you've made it to the end of the book, I'm going to assume that you've been able to access more pleasure in your life (or a certain state that brings you pleasure—calm, joy, excitement or freedom). So this chapter will help you ensure that that pleasure isn't fleeting; it will give you a really powerful tool to anchor it in, so that you can call on that state as you desire. You'll learn how to create triggers to your pleasure state so that it can be repeated, without needing to recreate the stimulus that generated the pleasure in the first place.

Think of it as an artificially induced state of pleasure that YOU get to consciously create for yourself, as you please.

When Mary arrives in Athens, she feels the 'pulse of her soul'. Arriving in Athens is the anchor; the state it elicits is the pulse of her soul.

When my husband brings me a coffee in bed while I'm bobbin' the babe in the morning, it makes me feel loved, supported and a bit mushy. The anchor is the coffee brought to me by my hubs; the state is loved, supported and a bit mushy. If I wanted to feel loved, supported and a bit mushy all the time, I could ask my husband to bring me coffee in bed all the time. (Just me?)

The thing is, we might not be able to constantly holiday in Athens, or get coffee in bed all day long. But we created that feeling within our body, so we can experience it again in our body, either with or without the original stimulus.

A MOTHER'S PLEASURE

For Mary, that picture of the church was one of the stimuli she was able to use to tap into the feeling of being in Athens—without having to be in Athens. And the more she repeated this process of experiencing the pulse of her soul, the more she anchored it into looking at this picture.

So what I'm sharing with you here and inviting you to play with is that you can feel pleasure (or an associated state of being) by consciously setting up your own anchors that will link to pleasure (or your desired state). You don't need to rely on holidaying in Athens to feel alive, or receiving coffees in bed to feel loved. You can set up an anchor in these moments—in the recreated moment or the imagined moment—to trigger the state you desire whenever you like.

It is so powerful and liberating to know that you can create a state or feeling on your own without relying on any external stimulus. Without requiring someone to do something for you. Without needing to travel anywhere (quite convenient for a lot of us in the global pandemic, especially if we have little ones in tow). You can begin to create an anchor that is accessible to you always.

There are three states we can choose from to set up anchors in:

1. The naturally occurring state. (The most powerful at creating an anchor.)
2. The recalled state. (The next most powerful.)
3. The imagined state. (The least powerful.)

It's easiest to set an anchor in the naturally occurring state, as you're feeling the pleasure directly and in the moment.

So if I want to set up an anchor of feeling loved, the best time for me to do that is during the rush of love I feel as I'm receiving that coffee from my husband in bed after being woken a thousand times the night before.

If he no longer brought me coffees in bed because he was on the morning shift for work or something, I could still elicit a sense of feeling loved by recalling the times that he had brought me coffees in bed previously—as I would be recalling the loved feeling in my mind.

If I wanted to set up an anchor for a state that I'd never actually experienced before, I wouldn't have the naturally occurring or recalled state available to me, so I would need to imagine the state and fire off the anchor when the desired feeling reached its peak.

Activity
Set your anchor

Begin by considering what would you like more of, or what else would you like to happen or experience, in your life right now, and let's create an anchor for it. To actually set up the anchor, here are the super simple but powerful steps I invite you to take:

1. Either in the natural, recalled or imagined state, find yourself at the peak of the state or feeling you desire.
2. When you're at the peak state, 'fire off' the

anchor, ideally for five to fifteen seconds; this can be achieved with a specific word, sound, touch or smell, or a combination of these (read on for more examples).
3. Repeatedly fire off this anchor as often as possible—either in the naturally occurring, recalled or imagined state—to increase its power.
4. Fire off the anchor outside of that state to evaluate whether it reproduces the desired feeling. Repeat steps 1–3 until this test works.

Your anchor can be anything that involves the senses. (Considering you're already experienced at being present and summoning your sensuality, this will be easy for you.) It could be:

- Visual—seeing your screensaver, a picture, a tattoo or an affirmation.
- Auditory—the sound of a singing bowl, a particular song, sound or theme tune.
- Olfactory—smelling an essential oil, cream, or flower.
- Kinaesthetic—touching, tapping or stroking a part of your body, receiving a certain touch from someone else, lighting a candle, clicking your fingers, clapping your hands.
- Gustatory—consuming a certain food or

drink.

It's also a good time to note that it's best to choose an anchor that is appropriate for the desired outcome. For example: if I want to elicit a feeling of peace when my kids are arguing with each other, screaming would not be the best anchor to choose.

I will share with you what we did in the example of my client, Mary, who wanted to re-experience the feeling she got from being in Athens.

Mary chose to anchor that feeling by becoming present at the peak of those feelings when she looked at that picture, then tapping on her heart. So every time she looked at the Athens picture, she tapped her heart to the point where the feelings of being alive and feeling the 'pulse' of her soul were associated with that action. Now she is able to elicit those feelings—whether she is in Athens or not, whether she is looking at the church picture or not—simply by tapping on her heart.

Ignite your desire

Maybe you'd like to set up an anchor for feeling turned on so that you can call on this sensation whenever you please; the first and most potent state in which to anchor your turn-on is in the moments and experiences where you're naturally turned on.

The more you can repeat this process, whether it be in the natural, recalled or imagined state (or a combination of the three: e.g. using the natural state when you're in a turned-on experience and the recalled state in between those experiences), the more you will anchor it. Daily would be ideal.

If, for example, you want to elicit your turn-on because it feels like your libido has disappeared, and you're really missing sexual intimacy with your partner because you usually 'just don't feel like it', you can begin to explore and experience anything that makes you feel turned on, and build your anchor from there.

(Note: This wouldn't be the first or only thing I'd advise friends or clients to do when it comes to a lack of desire. If they're in the early postpartum phase or similar, they might find that they do have desire, but in this season of life it is more of a desire for rest, healing and intimacy with themselves and their baby.)

About a year after one of my clients, Ashley, had had her second child, she realised that she was craving sexual excitement and arousal; that turned-on feeling she used to share with her husband. The times that they were able to have sexual intimacy with each other in that season of parenting and family life were in tiny little windows, and she admitted they often skipped a lot of actual arousal before having penetrative sex.

So to ignite her arousal and set an anchor for it, Ashley and her partner spent their next days generating arousal and sexual energy, with no intention of penetrative sex or climax. They explored what worked for her in terms of redefining her desire, summoning her sensuality and having open, honest communication with each other. They went about it like a playful, intimacy-building experiment to discover what turned her on, and then she went to work creating her arousal anchor.

Some of the activities that they explored in this experiment included:

- talking about their desires
- holding each other
- hugging
- kissing
- massaging
- exploring sensuality in and out of bed
- swapping phones for candlelight at night
- lots of play—including flirtatious play that they hadn't engaged in in a long time

Ashley was consciously seeking her arousal and looking for the evidence of it. And when she noticed it, she went deeper into it; during peak times of arousal, Ashley would consciously activate her 'arousal trigger' by running her hand over her right thigh, until it became a set anchor.

So now, when she wants to feel turned on, Ashley fires her anchor by rubbing her right thigh, and experiences the electrical current of arousal beginning to strum her body.

Being in control of our own arousal—using it to enjoy time on our own or with a partner, or to generate a surge of electricity in our bodies to connect us with the ecstasy of life—is one of the greatest powers to possess.

A MOTHER'S PLEASURE

The benefit of anchoring pleasure is that as you continue to be open to, seek, find, create, receive and experience pleasure in your life, you also get to savour it and replicate it as you please, even in the least pleasurable moments.

You can create an anchor that is accessible to you, always.

Chapter fourteen
MAMA EROS

Show me the mother who can subtly command a room, who is magnetic and alluring and inspiring, simply from showing up in her true essence.

Show me the mother who glows, who seems to move through her days with feel-good flow.

Show me the mother who radiates light from under her skin, whose lips curl up at the side because she knows some kind of unicorn-mother secret.

Show me the mother who is connected to her partner by more than their offspring; by an alive, electrical current.

Show me the mother who feels alive, connected and ecstatic, and she will show you what it's like to prioritise your pleasure.

She will show you what it's like to not be consumed with madness and frustration at the children she adores and devotes her everything to.

She will show you what it looks like to be a conduit for the pulse of life's pleasure current, for the current of electric eros, Mama Eros.

She will show you what it is to be a goddess embodied—without needing to be barefoot and braided, adorned in floaty florals.

She is not some mythical creature, even though it might be hard to believe she's real. She is no more special than you or I, or any other mother in line at the coffee shop or grocery store.

She is likely going to trigger the shit out of every mother who hasn't felt the natural feminine force of Mama Eros; even just the description of her on this page might create resistance to her from within you.

Because when we first opened this book, we couldn't have imagined how she was possible.

Because with all the roles we've taken on that society offered us, this role was not on the list.

But she gets to be alive for you, because she *is* you.

She is within you

The discomfort we feel when we witness a mother in her unapologetic aliveness and deep connection to self belongs to all of us. Our discomfort is not a demand for her to be less; our discomfort is a call for us to reclaim her for ourselves. To reintegrate that part of ourselves and return to wholeness—a place where making art of the clouds with our children, experiencing ecstasy from the twirl of a toddler's curl around our finger, or surrendering to sacred moments with ourselves or a partner, reminds us that our power to be present and enjoy this life is already available to us. We don't need to buy or earn it; it's ours.

Being connected to your eros—your erotic, ecstatic nature—may have seemed so far out of reach for you before you began to journey with this book. I wonder if you're starting to feel Mama Eros somewhere inside of you? I wonder if you can start to hear her whispers reminding you to dance, asking you to accept and receive, inviting you back home to yourself through pleasure.

Why couldn't she be you? Ask yourself now—*why can't this woman, humming a resonant full-body thrum, be me?*

She is there within you. She already is you; you already are her.

Not once you've lost the weight, not once the kids are older, not once you can finally have a romantic weekend away, not once you've got new non-maternity bras or a new wardrobe—now.

She lives inside of you. And the last piece of the puzzle to reclaiming her, that I want to share with you here, is reclaiming her erotic nature.

The erotic nature that perhaps made her become a mother in the first place. The erotic nature that has her electrified by life. The erotic nature that she's been conditioned to suppress.

Reclaim your eros

A mother kept from her eros is a mother more subservient

to a society that prioritises patriarchy and keeps the cogs of a capitalist economy turning.

When seeking eroticism, the last place most will look is within motherhood. The idea that a mother could be turned on, and claim and express her desire, is something our society rejects and disapproves of.

And does it serve her? No.

Does it serve her partner? No.

Does it serve her children, her community or this world into which she birthed life? Fuck no.

It is time we reclaimed our eros. For better or worse. Through pandemics and in health. Until death separates us from her, because a woman disconnected from her eros, from her pleasure, is a death in itself.

The grace of it all

There will be no rituals, practices or prompts in this chapter. Just a few moments in time where you get to look back at what you've traversed. A chapter where you get to land in your body and have reverence for all that your body is for you. For all that it connects you with. A moment where you can realise your personal power to change the unconscious undercurrent of your mind, welcome the wellspring of your emotions, lay it all down in front of you and see with your own eyes the glory of it all.

We've had our eros deemed disgraceful for long enough; it's time to revel in the grace of it all.

So how do we do this?

There is nothing required for this reclamation. Except

for you to feel it. To see it. To hear, smell and taste it. To choose it. To know it as wisdom that resides inside you—wisdom that you get to pass on to your sons and daughters through living it. To receive the pulse of it through your body as the creative, feminine frequency that is your birthright. You are alive in this body that allows you to live, so do just that and live your Mama Eros.

Smell the roses. Kiss your partner. Feel the moments of bliss dancing in your kitchen as your baby shuffles towards you. Relish in the moments of laughter as you and your partner giggle under the sheets, trying not to wake the baby. Melt from the warmth of your children in the early hours. Surrender to the queen that is within you, asking you to fuck the playdough off and slip into a pair of heels.

Surrender yourself to the pleasure of it all.

For I am a pleasure genie and I am offering you pleasure in every moment of every day, forever and ever.

Do you choose to receive it?

She is within you.
She is you;
you are her.

Resources

There are so many great resources out there to explore pleasure, desire, self-discovery and personal growth. This is a list I've found helpful or have contributed within these pages in some form or another. It is in no way an exhaustive list of what I've drawn on over the years of pleasure exploration, but they are my most favourite or most appropriate to list given the content in this book.

Books

Tao Tantric Arts for Women: Cultivating Sexual Energy, Love, and Spirit
Minke de Vos

Come as You Are: The Surprising New Science That Will Transform Your Sex Life
Emily Nagoski

Healing Love through the Tao Cultivating Female Sexual Energy
Mantak Chia

The Gifts of Imperfection: Let Go of Who You Think You're Supposed to Be and Embrace Who You Are
Brené Brown

Of Woman Born: Motherhood as Experience and Institution
Adrienne Rich

Pussy: A Reclamation
Regena Thomashauer

The Gorgeous Revolution
Dee Light

The Wild Woman's Way: Unlock Your Full Potential for Pleasure, Power, and Fulfillment
Michaela Boehm

Breaking the Habit of Being Yourself: How to Lose Your Mind and Create a New One
Dr Joe Dispenza

How Pleasure Works: Why We Like What We Like
Paul Bloom

Mentors and others who've contributed to *A Mother's Pleasure* or my work:

Hayley Carr - Mindset shifting and all things Neurolinguistic Programming

Callie Brown - Self expression, clarity and connection
Carlie Maree - Book writing
Bonnie Bliss - Somatic Sexologist
Danielle Savory - Sex Coach for Women

Other Resources

Online resources by Layla Martin

Article: Babies bring abundance by Denise Duffield-Thomas

Quoted Glennon Doyle podcast, We Can Do Hard Things: episode 12 Parenting: How do we make this thrilling roller coaster ride a little bit easier?

Activity: Discerning Desire from chapter six, Redefine Desire. This is a practice that was shared with me by Diedre Light of Manifesto of Light, also the author of The Gorgeous Revolution.

Activity: The practice from chapter nine. The seven questions I invite you to ask were inspired, in part, by Byron Katie's The Four Questions.

Naked yoga class mentioned was facilitated by Rosie Rees: https://rosierees.com/

Conscious Parenting, previous course run by Bridget Wood and Julie Tenner from Nourishing the Mother

Acknowledgements

I would like to acknowledge the custodians of the land on which this book was written: specifically the Wodi Wodi people of Dharawal land on the south-east coast of Australia. This land has gifted me some of the peace, stillness, beauty and creativity I needed for this creation. I extend this acknowledgement to all Aboriginal and Torres Strait Islander persons who are reading *A Mother's Pleasure*.

So many incredible, talented and intelligent people have helped shape this book. Thank you to my publishing team who have made the process pleasurable. Natasha Gilmour for your unwavering and always soothing support. Thank you for seeing the power of this work, honouring my voice and holding me through the gestation and birth of this book with such integrity and professionalism. Thank you to the very talented Georgia for your masterful editing. I've become a better writer just from seeing your edits and receiving your suggestions. Chrysta, thank you for housing my words in such a divine cover design. Your design skill and patience is deeply appreciated.

I am deeply grateful for the privilege of being a mother,

for the lessons I've learned (and will continue to learn) and the experiences gifted to me by my three children, Zieke, Oscar and Thea. You have enabled me to fill the pages within this book, and every space within my heart. Thank you for setting me on the path of pleasure, for the opportunity to undergo personal growth at hyper-speed, and for keeping me humble. Thank you for your permission to share our stories and for being ridiculously cute, hilarious and entertaining along the way. Thank you for calling me into the joyous, pleasure-filled motherhood I hadn't known was possible until you all arrived. I will love you forever.

Jake, my husband, one love, and quiet couch companion to my writing of this book. Thank you for your unwavering support and for always saying yes to the left-of-field ideas I have; the hours to myself for work, writing or whatever the hell I want; and every new iteration of me as the full-spectrum woman I am. Without your support, my work and this book wouldn't be possible. Your dedication to me and our family means I can dedicate my time, energy and attention to this creation and show our children we can follow our desires and create change in our world. Thank you for sharing your beer, laughing with me, being by my side always and on top when it counts. You're a spunk and I'm so grateful for you. Love you, babe.

To my mum, Michelle—I've been blessed to have you as my mama. Thank you for always supporting me in everything that I do, and for never trying to change me from exactly the person I am. You've given me the confidence to live my life, do what I desire and be my pleasure-seeking self without fear of judgement or criticism from as early as I can remember. I appreciate all the times you've offered up your house as my co-work space for interviews or just a quiet space to work. Knowing you are always there for support has meant more to me than you know.

There are so many wise, inspiring and all-round glorious women who've helped me birth this book into the world in some way or another as friends and/or mentors—women with whom I've been fortunate enough to have conversations around pleasure, motherhood or writing and publishing. Who have held space for me to untangle my thoughts. Who have helped me be a better writer. Or who have simply encouraged me along the way when I've forgotten to encourage myself. This includes Kelly Ryan, Callie Brown, Kate Darnell, Carlie Maree, Belinda Hearn, Anna Murray, Sarah Nott and Tayma De Agnoli.

Thank you to the divine women who took time to read, critique and provide feedback and insights on the first draft. Melanie Dwarte, Mary Sotiros, Stephanie Meekings and Bianca Edgar—I truly value all of your input and am so grateful you said yes.

I want to thank the intelligent, masterful change-making women and leaders of their industry I had the privilege of interviewing for this book, including Bonnie Bliss, Danielle Savory and Hayley Carr. Thank you for your contributions to this book and the invaluable work you do in the world.

About the author

REGAN FIGG

Regan Figg is a pleasurepreneur and mum of three who mentors women to connect with their innate feminine wisdom and lead pleasure-filled lives.

In 2016, Regan was diagnosed with perinatal mood disorders during her son's first year earthside. As a former exercise physiologist, yoga and meditation teacher, and health and wellness coach, Regan was shocked at how much she struggled to look after herself in motherhood.

Today, Regan shares the invaluable tools she developed to not just cope in motherhood, but to relish it. Through one-on-one coaching, group journeys, her podcast The Pleasure Collective, and now her new book, Regan helps women to dispel societal conditioning, reclaim their goddess energy, and create feel-good flow in motherhood.

A Mother's Pleasure is Regan's first book.

Keep opening (to pleasure)
Thank you for including me and this book in your exploration of pleasure in motherhood. I would be honoured to continue to support you along your pathway to pleasure.

Go deeper
If you liked this book and want to go deeper, check out my offerings at reganfigg.com/offerings

Get close
To receive updates on what I'm sharing, exploring, loving as well as free teachings and gifts, sign up to my newsletter at reganfigg.com/signup

Stay in touch
Website: reganfigg.com
Instagram: @Regan_Figg
Facebook: @TheReganFigg

www.ingramcontent.com/pod-product-compliance
Lightning Source LLC
Chambersburg PA
CBHW020320010526
44107CB00054B/1916